NADIA G'S
Bitchin' Kitchen
COOKIN'
FOR TROUBLE

WRITTEN BY: NADIA G

CREATED BY: NADIA G & JOSHUA DORSEY

BALLANTINE BOOKS TRADE PAPERBACKS
NEW YORK

A BALLANTINE BOOKS TRADE PAPERBACK ORIGINAL

COPYRIGHT © 2011 BY NADIA GIOSIA
FOREWORD COPYRIGHT © 2011 BY GUY FIERI

ALL RIGHTS RESERVED.

PUBLISHED IN THE UNITED STATES BY BALLANTINE BOOKS, AN IMPRINT
OF THE RANDOM HOUSE PUBLISHING GROUP,
A DIVISION OF RANDOM HOUSE, INC.,NEW YORK.

BALLANTINE AND COLOPHON ARE REGISTERED TRADEMARKS OF RANDOM HOUSE, INC

GRATEFUL ACKNOWLEDGMENT IS MADE OF SKIRT!, A DIVISION OF GLOBE PEQUOT
PRESS, FOR PERMISSION TO REPRINT TEXT FROM *BITCHIN' KITCHEN COOKBOOK:
ROCK YOUR KITCHEN — AND LET THE BOYS CLEAN UP THE MESS* BY NADIA G,
COPYRIGHT © 2009 BY B360 MEDIA, INC. USED BY PERMISSION OF SKIRT!, A DIVISION
OF GLOBE PEQUOT PRESS, GUILFORD, CT USA.

ISBN 978-0-345-53182-7
eISBN 978-0-345-53183-4

PRINTED IN THE UNITED STATES OF AMERICA ON ACID-FREE PAPER

WWW.BALLANTINEBOOKS.COM

9 8 7 6 5 4 3 2 1

FIRST EDITION

DESIGNED BY: NADIA G

THIS BOOK IS DEDICATED TO:
THE BITCHIN' FAMIGLIA

contents

Foreword by: GUY FIERI

When I was a kid, growing up in a small Northern California town, Ferndale, my parents were kind of on the hippie fringe, especially when it came to food…tofu, quinoa, and a bunch of other stuff that doesn't exactly excite a kid. And I wanted to eat…chicken parm, ribeye steaks, salami, etc. As they often do, my parents gave it to me straight: "Guy, if you want to eat it, you can make it yourself." So, at about ten years old, I hit the local butcher shop, bought a couple of steaks and cooked 'em up. My dad cut into it, took a bite and kind of gave me this look. "Oh boy, am I gonna get it now!" I thought, but he turned to me and said, "Guy, this might just be the best steak I've ever had." And that was it. I knew what I wanted to do. Cooking those steaks for my family was the beginning of my own personal Food Revolution and I never looked back.

All that I ever wanted to be was a good dad, a chef, and own my own restaurant. And by the time I was twenty-five, I was on the road to both. Hunter was just born and two months later, we opened my first restaurant, Johnny Garlic's California Pasta Grill. The confluence of food and fatherhood was so obvious to me at that point that I knew I was on the right path. Teaching people about good food and providing them a satisfying and enjoyable experience was my MO both at work and at home. My message was becoming more and more clear. My Food Revolution.

By the time I won *The Next Food Network Star* in 2005, I was already pretty much set and happy in my life: TV was the last thing I thought I'd be doing…let alone food TV. But my buddies told me I'd be good so I gave it a shot and the rest is history. Celebrity chef, culinary rockstar, TV host, *New York Times* bestselling author, whatever people try to label me, my message remains the same. My personal goals and my Food Revolution are still consistent and I just look at it like I've got a bigger platform to spread the message.

Mentors like my buddy Emeril made a big impact on me in my first TV years and gave me the confidence to push forward with my message, even when people wanted to hear other things from me. People always want me to talk about whatever giant sandwich I ate on the road with *Diners, Drive-ins, and Dives*. But what I want to tell them about is how important it is to get off the couch and into the kitchen with their kids to teach them the all-important life skill of cooking. I want them to know how to avoid childhood obesity by teaching their kids the basics of nutrition and cooking whole foods as opposed to processed foods. I want them to know that spending time in the kitchen with their kids will give the next generation more confidence and a more positive affirmation than they can imagine. I want people to see the connection between moderation, exercise, and careful attention to what we put in our bodies. That's the real Guy Fieri. That's my Food Revolution.

When I first met my paisan Nadia G and watched her show, *Bitchin' Kitchen,* I saw a kindred spirit. She's totally out of bounds and follows her own rules. I read her first book cover to cover and couldn't believe what she was pullin' off! And I knew she was really onto something when even my dad came to me and told me he'd read the whole book…I didn't think that it would be up his alley at all. But, you never know what audience you can reach when you are pushing the envelope. Nadia didn't have a TV platform so she invented her own medium online. My way of speaking to people has always been through my restaurants, my food, and now my shows. Nadia's is through her passionate online community and now, TV. We reach people in different ways but I see the focus and drive she has to communicate with her people. *Cookin' for Trouble* is passionate and hilarious but most important, it's full of great recipes from growing up in her Italian family.

Nadia can cook and Nadia can tell a story and when it comes to communicating with people, that's what you need. Nadia's got her own revolution going on and I dig that. She's got a lot to say and she won't stop until you hear it. The message is in her kitchen that's Bitchin' and she's Cookin' for Trouble. — Guy (Guido)

Introduction

Some of the best meals I've ever eaten weren't concocted in 5-star restaurants. In fact, they were created by people who've never even heard of a Michelin star. These cooks didn't graduate from Le Cordon Bleu, the Culinary Institute of America, or the Academy of *Stu Cazze. The best meals I've ever eaten were made by humble folks who'd probably clothesline whoever invented the decorative rosemary sprig. I'm talking about Mom, *Nonna, *Zia, Cugi…

It's from that long line of bad-ass, home-schooled, fierce-female cooks that I learned to dish it out. And I ain't just talkin' food. See, in my family, the kitchen was where it all went down. It's where we laughed, confessed, brawled, celebrated, and mourned. We practically lived in the kitchen, and that's definitely where we came alive. Food just set the stage…until it was time to eat, then "Shaddup and pass da Parmigiano," but you get the picture.

And that's how we roll on *Bitchin' Kitchen*. We're loud, we're messy, and we've got a meal for every occasion. From "Breakup Brunches" to "Dysfunctional Family Pizza Night," we're not afraid to lay it all on the table, laugh in the face of whatever life serves up, and stuff our gullets while we're at it. As fresh as this concept may seem, it's actually pretty old school. And I guess that's why we have the most Bitchin' community in the lifestyle space. Because ultimately, we're like family (or the family you never wished you had) — breaking bread, breaking balls, and breaking all the rules.

People always ask me where I got the idea for a "crazy comedy-cooking show." Easy: I grew up in a crazy comedy-cooking show. What I wonder is where people got the idea that the kitchen was some kinda sterile space with about as much personality as a stainless countertop? *Boh. I don't know about you, but the kitchens I grew up in were beautifully chaotic, and that's exactly how I like it.

So it's time to take back the kitchen, Ladies and Ginos. Get your hands dirty. Make a mess. Trade that cardigan for some stilettos, and have some freakin' fun! Because if you ain't having fun, you ain't gonna cook. And if you ain't cookin', a lot more than your stomach can go hungry. As the old Italian saying goes: "The family that eats together, digests together." What? I told you the saying was old, not deep.

Let's Get Cooking.

The Bitchin' Crew

THE SPICE AGENT

Meet Yeres…Yirisk…ah f@ck it…The Spice Agent is *Bitchin' Kitchen*'s dark and mildy mysterious spice specialist. He hails from Raanana, where the world's best spices are grown. To get there: exit Ben Gurion, pass Kfar Saba, turn right, turn left, you can't miss it.

PANOS THE FISH 'N' MEAT GUY

Panos is our Greek fishmonger and butcher. His family has been in the meat business for generations: His father was a meat guy, his grandmother was a meat guy, even his great grandfather was… oh never mind, he was just an asshole. The point is, when it comes to expertly knowing critters (and how to get that "wet look" with hair gel), Panos is the master of disaster, *bro.

HANS
THE SCANTILY CLAD
FOOD CORRESPONDENT

Hans may be greased up and chiseled, but don't let his magical sheen fool you into thinking he's mere eye candy. Not only is Hans our resident nutritionist, but he's also the respected inventor of a patented workout system that targets three major muscle groups through five sets of fifteen reps. He calls it: "Three Major Muscle Groups Targeted by Five Sets of Fifteen Reps." Yea.

The BITCHIN' KITCHEN CODE

FEARLESSNESS Every time I get a new knife or grater or use any sharp metal kitchen contraption for the first time, I get cut. So will you. Be prepared to get spritzed with hot oil, scalded with boiling water, suffer second-degree burns from cast-iron pans… but don't fret, pretty soon you won't feel it anymore and your tough hands will become a badge of honor…or a gnarled mess, whatever.

PATIENCE Take the time to julienne the peppers, cube the potatoes, mince the garlic, make a freakin' basil chiffonade. Straight guys are especially bad at this, "A potato is a potato, just rub it on your T-shirt, peel off a few strands of skin and slap it in the pan, right?" Wrong. All these little prep steps are super important: not only do they affect cook-time, but ingredients are passive-aggressive: If you don't pay attention to them, they'll get you back when dinner is served. *Hisss.*

CREATIVITY In the culinary world nothing is written in stone. If a recipe calls for a big pinch of sugar, you may like two or none at all. So always taste as you go, involve yourself with the different layers of flavor, make adjustments, make it yours. Unless you have really bad taste — then just follow the directions.

RESPECT To make a good meal, you need good ingredients. I buy all organic, but there are a few ingredients that REALLY should be organic: meat and dairy. I know, organic meat is expensive, but it's supposed to be. It's easy to forget, but that juicy steak used to be a live animal that needed food, shelter, and water itself — for years — before blossoming into dinner. In life, there's no such thing as a free lunch. If you're buying cheap meat, you're getting a lot more than you bargained for: antibiotics, growth hormones, a daughter getting her period before the age of ten thanks to all of the above…Same goes with dairy. Anyways, we all know that cutting down on meat and dairy is healthy. So long story longer: buy better meat, and eat less of it. I'd rather own two pairs of D&G heels than twenty pairs of pleather monstrocities.

LOVE Cheesy as it may sound, it's true. The more you watch a sauce, fuss, and carefully stir, the better it tastes. (Psst. If anyone asks, I didn't tell you this.)

Nadia G's Accent

Many have wondered where my accent comes from: New Jersey? Brooklyn? Russia, perhaps? While some asked questions, others sent hate mail. They couldn't place my accent, and that made them mad. These flustered knights of knowledge demanded "the truth" and would not rest until my accent was "debunked"… or their meds kicked in. So here's the 411:

My parents emigrated from Italy to Montreal, Quebec, in the 1950s. My father came from Guglionesi, Campobasso, where they speak a dialect of 'Mulise.' My mom hails from Torrice, a small town in Frosinone, where they speak their own dialect of "Ciociaro."

Fast forward a coupla decades, and I was born in Montreal, Quebec, a French-Canadian city. But make no mistake, the French spoken in Montreal is a far cry from the guttural French you'll hear in France. "Quebecois" is to European French what the Southern Drawl is to British English. Onwards.

When I was little, I was raised speaking Italian. I then went to English school, but took quite a few bilingual courses (that's how we roll in Mtl). And to this day, I speak three languages: English, French, and Italian. I also pretend to speak Spanish, when in fact I'm speaking Italian.

Now, here's the kicker: I grew up in St. Leonard, an Italian neighborhood where folks don't just have a peculiar Italian-Montreal accent, they created a whole freakin' language, *bro! A dialect which is colorful and cringe-worthy. St. Leonard is a town where backyards aren't gardens, they're tomato factories. It's a town where Civics are the vehicle of choice, and "Rhythm Is a Dancer" blasts through the souped-up speakers (…which are worth more than the car). It's a town where people named Joe, Mary, Tina, and Gino eat cutlet "sangwiches" and live with their parents until they're 40. Where the boys are clean shaven, and in certain cases I wish we could say the same for the girls.

Anyways, the point is, when I speak you'll hear glimmers of these influences: French, Italian, "St. Leonard-ese," depending on how flustered I am. And sometimes, if you listen really closely, you can also hear dolphins cry. It's a beautiful thing.

nadvice

Whenever you come across "St. Leonardese" in this book, you can turn to page 194 for the Italian slang dictionary, *capisce?

(dysfunctional) family pizza night

I have such fond memories of pizza night. The family sitting around the table. Dad pitching salami at me: *"Catch it in your mouth Nadia! COME ON! WHADDYA GOOD FOR?!"* Mom screeching: *"Stop it, Joe! She's not a cat!"* Bah. Whether you're throwing things at each other or yelling in the name of conversation, pizza night is a sacred tradition that's guaranteed to bring your family and thighs closer together.

Now, when most people think of authentic Italian pizza, they usually envision thin-crust, wood-fired pies. But my family never made it this way. Why? Well, the lack of a wood-burning oven is one reason. But the way *we* *shkoff, those wimpy pizzas are an appetizer at best. So my family started making big pizzas, rustic pan pizzas, and the time's come for me to pass down the Giosia secret recipe.

But when it comes to family, a lot more than recipes get passed down, and it ain't always tasty. Like annoying habits. Take my mom, for example. She always manages to see the negative side of things. This lady doesn't plan for retirement, she plans for losing her job due to a crippling illness caused by a third World War, and *"Oh no what's Nadia gonna eat?!"* And guess what? As I got older, I started doing the same freakin' thing, always seeing the bad side. But with therapy, I've managed to nip it right in the bud. Now anytime I see the glass half empty, I immediately fill it with chardonnay. Cheers. Let's get cooking.

nadvice

Let your kids choose their own toppings. So what if you're not a fan of chocolate and salami? It's all about empowering your *shquiblets. See, if you always micro-manage your kids' lives, you end up breeding out the traits you admire most in adults: independence, confidence, creativity... So let go, start small, and give them the power to choose their own ingredients. (Except peas. Cam'an, you can't put peas on a pizza. *Pfft.*)

zia mimi's pizza dough

This recipe makes a focaccia-like dough. But there are *all kinds of different pizza doughs out there. For example in Napoli, they have one style that's soft and loose like naan bread. This way they can fold the pizza into quarters and *shkoff it a *libretto,* which means "book-style pizza." I guess these Italians thought a folded pizza resembled a book, and hence the downfall of the Italian economy.

servings: dough for 1 large pizza | easy

SHKIAFFING IT TOGETHER

Mix the yeast with the warm water in a medium-sized bowl and let it sit for 5 minutes. Then add 2 tablespoons of extra-virgin olive oil, raw sugar, and sea salt. Whisk and set aside. In a large bowl, sift together the all-purpose and whole-wheat flour. Make a well in the center of the flour, and pour in the yeast mixture. Using your hands, mix in the flour until all the liquid is absorbed. Now sprinkle a clean surface with flour and knead the dough until it's smooth. If the dough is too sticky, add some more flour as needed. Once it's smooth, shape the dough into a ball.

Coat a large ceramic bowl with a tablespoon of extra-virgin olive oil. Place the dough in the ceramic bowl, and flip it over a few times to lightly coat the dough with oil. Loosely cover the top of the dough with plastic wrap, and completely cover the top of the ceramic bowl with a dish towel. Let it rise for 2 hours, until the dough has doubled in size. Then punch down the dough, and let it rise for another hour.

GROCERY LIST

- *1 tsp active dry yeast*
- *1¼ cups warm water*
- *3 tbsp extra-virgin olive oil*
- *1 tsp raw sugar*
- *1 tsp sea salt*
- *1 cup all-purpose flour, plus extra for kneading*
- *1 cup whole-wheat flour*

GEAR

- *medium mixing bowl*
- *large mixing bowl*
- *large ceramic bowl*

"Did you know that there are more than 1,500 species of yeast, which is only 1% of all yeasty species thought to exist?! This is one of those 'funny facts' to tell your children on family pizza night. Another 'funny fact' is that yeast and parents have one major thing in common — they both reproduce asexually."

pizza con le patate

I first tasted this potato pizza at my aunt Carmela's house. There were a buncha "firsts" at Zia Carmela's house — like tasting a habañero (at the age of four). Or watching a pig being gutted in a family vacation video. The potato pizza compensated, though…I think.

servings: 6 to 8 | easy

THE CRUST

Preheat the oven to 475°F, and place the oven rack at the bottom. Grease a pizza pan generously with the leaf lard. Work the dough to fit the pan. Brush the top of the dough with 1 tablespoon of extra-virgin olive oil. Place the pizza crust in the oven, and cook for 5 minutes to pre-crisp.

THE TOPPINGS

Using a mandoline, slice the potatoes and onion paper-thin. Remove the leaves from the rosemary sprigs and set them aside, discarding the stalks.

SHKIAFFING IT TOGETHER

Take the pizza crust out of the oven, and add 2 layers of potatoes in a scalloped pattern. On top of the potatoes add a layer of onion, and sprinkle with the rosemary leaves. Drizzle with the remaining olive oil, and sprinkle with the sea salt and the freshly cracked black pepper. Cook for 8 more minutes or until the potatoes have golden, crispy edges.

GROCERY LIST

- *2 tbsp leaf lard*
- *1 batch pizza dough (see page 5)*
- *3 to 4 tbsp extra-virgin olive oil*
- *3 russet potatoes*
- *1 Vidalia onion*
- *2 fresh rosemary sprigs*
- *1 tsp sea salt*
- *freshly cracked black pepper, to taste*

GEAR

- *13" x 18" pizza pan*
- *mandoline*

all-dressed g-style pizza

This all-dressed pizza rocks: salty salame di Genoa, tangy kalamata olives, a sweet n' spicy tomato sauce, and just enough fresh baby spinach to make you feel like you're eating healthy :P.

servings: 6 to 8 | easy

TOMATO SAUCE

In a large bowl, hand-crushed tomatoes. Add the olive oil, garlic, fresh basil, parsley, dried basil, dried oregano, chile flakes, Parmigiano, sea salt, and lots of cracked black pepper. Mix. Cover and let it sit in the fridge for 3 hours, or overnight.

SHKIAFFING IT TOGETHER

Preheat the oven to 475°F, placing the oven rack at the bottom. Grease the pizza pan with the leaf lard and work the dough to fit the pan. Spread ¼ cup of the sauce over the dough. Place the pizza crust in the oven, and cook for 5 minutes to pre-crisp.

After 5 minutes, take the pizza out and add another ¼ cup of sauce. Place the pizza crust back into the oven and cook for another 5 minutes. (We want the crust to develop some backbone, so it can handle all the toppings.)

Take the pizza out again, and add your toppings: 1 layer of mozzarella rounds, sprinkle with the pecorino, and add the salame strips and kalamata olives. Put the pizza back in the oven and cook for a final 5 minutes.

Imediately remove it from the pan, and sprinkle with the julienned baby spinach.

GROCERY LIST

- 1½ cups canned San Marzano plum tomatoes
- 3 tbsp extra-virgin olive oil
- 2 garlic cloves, minced
- 4 fresh basil leaves, torn
- ¼ cup flat-leaf parsley, minced
- ½ tsp dried basil
- ½ tsp dried Greek oregano
- ¼ tsp hot chile flakes
- 1 tbsp finely grated Parmigiano
- ¼ tsp sea salt
- freshly cracked black pepper, to taste
- 2 tbsp leaf lard
- 1 batch pizza dough (see page 5)
- 1 lb fresh buffalo mozzarella, sliced into ¼"-thick rounds
- ½ cup grated pecorino cheese
- ¼ lb salame di genoa, cut into strips
- ½ cup marinated kalamata olives, pitted and halved
- ½ cup julienned fresh baby spinach

GEAR

- large mixing bowl
- 13" x 18" pizza pan (round pan is optional)

puttanesca panzarottis

You know what's even better than homemade pizza? Deep-fried homemade pizza.

servings: 10 to 12 panzarottis | easy

PIZZA SAUCE

Use a fine wire-mesh sieve to drain all the liquid from the tomato sauce. Roughly chop the drained tomato chunks into little pieces, and set aside.

DOUGH

Dust a clean surface with flour. Roll out the dough ⅛ inch thick. If the dough is too sticky, dust with more flour. Once the dough is rolled out, use the cookie cutter to cut out 10 to 12 circles of dough. On one half of each circle, place 1 tablespoon of mozzarella, 1 tablespoon of drained tomato pieces, ¼ teaspoon of capers, and 1 chopped anchovy, and sprinkle with 1 teaspoon of Romano cheese. Fold the circle over, and completely seal the edges with a fork.

SHKIAFFING IT TOGETHER

In a heavy pot, heat 6 inches of vegetable oil to 350°F on the thermometer. Deep-fry each panzarotti until golden, crispy, and cooked through, 5 to 7 minutes. Place them on paper towels to drain the excess oil.

GROCERY LIST

- 1 batch tomato sauce (see page 9)
- all-purpose flour, for dusting
- 1 batch pizza dough (see page 5)
- ¾ cup diced mozzarella
- 2 tbsp capers
- 10 canned anchovies, drained and chopped
- ⅓ cup grated Romano cheese
- vegetable oil, for deep-frying

GEAR

- fine wire-mesh sieve
- rolling pin
- 5" round cookie cutter
- heavy pot (for deep-frying)
- deep-frying thermometer

nadvice

As a variation, try stuffing the panzarottis with creamy goat cheese and pitted ripe Bing cherries. Or what about crumbled feta and baby spinach sautéed in garlic and lemon juice? The only ingredient that doesn't work as a stuffing is oil, so make sure you seal these babies tight.

frittelle

"Frittelle" — Italian donuts. Wherever there's homemade pizza, there's frittelle. Why? Well, Italians are so cheap that they won't let an '80s hair style go to waste, never mind pizza dough. So the leftover dough is fried, and traditionally served with sugar for dipping. But we're taking it to the next level and also serving it up with chocolate nougat fondue.

servings: 12 frittelle | easy

CHOCOLATE NOUGAT FONDUE

Heat a double boiler over medium heat. Add the bittersweet chocolate, Toblerone, and cream to the top pan. Stir until all the chocolate has melted.

SHKIAFFING IT TOGETHER

Heat 6 inches of canola oil in a large heavy pot to 350°F on the thermometer. Shape the pizza dough into fingers, about 4 inches long and ½ inch thick. Deep-fry in small batches for 4 to 5 minutes, until golden and cooked through. Drain on a wire rack. Serve with a bowl of raw sugar for dipping, and another bowl of the chocolate nougat fondue.

GROCERY LIST

- ½ cup chopped bittersweet chocolate
- 2 cups chopped Toblerone candy
- ½ cup half & half
- canola oil, for deep-frying
- 1 batch pizza dough (see page 5)
- ½ cup raw sugar, for dipping

GEAR

- double boiler
- large heavy pot
- deep-frying thermometer

"For da record, I'm not into 'Family Pizza Nite'. Why? Because EVERY NITE IS FAMILY NITE at the Panagiotiskoussioulas household! Dat's right, every single nite we sit down and eat togedder: me, my wife, our baby boy Vasilios, my mother, her mother, my grandfather, my third cousin, my uncle visiting from Mikonos, and his two Pomeranians, *bro…*"

student shkoff-fest

*B*eing a student ain't easy. From budgets as small as your dorm room to "finding yourself"… passed out with a beer hat and one sock, I feel your pain. That's why in this chapter we're serving up a Bitchin' College Survival Guide, complete with one-pot meals you can cook on a freakin' hot plate. So, if you're a student (…or just a "student of life" hiding from the law in a cheap motel room) — this chapter's for *YOU*!

Man, I'll never forget my first week in college: all those new faces, intense lectures…I remember saying to myself: "F@#k this, I'll take my chances on the Web." But that's not the point. The point is: between exams, hangovers, and all that armchair activism, you ain't eating right! In fact, you may even have scurvy.

Scurvy = not good. So let's yap a bit about the importance of cooking for yourself in college. Sure it's healthy, blah blah blah. But more important, it gives you a competitive advantage in the relationship department! Let's call a spade a *newrd here — as a student you're not exactly a "prime catch": no money, no pad…Man, you probably even stopped wearing deodorant in the name of feminism or something. BUT, if you can cook up a Bitchin' meal, now that gives you something more to offer than an "ironic" T-shirt and a half-baked conspiracy theory, *capiche*? Good. Let's get cooking.

One of the hardest parts about being a student is choosing a career, so here's some Nadvice for ya: Whatever you do, don't listen to your parents. Seriously. Eh, Mom & Dad: if you're so passionate about chartered accounting, it's never too late to take a class. As for all the youngsters — do what YOU love to do, and the money will come…maybe.

⚠ WARNING: *Bitchin' Kitchen is not responsible for inspiring financially fruitless degrees. These BAs may include, but are not limited to, Philosophy, Fine Arts, Women's Studies, and Experimental Film.*

University at

Bachelor of Fine Arts

has been granted this

thai green curry w/ eggplant + udon

When you need energy, there's nothing like a big bowl of spicy noodles. As the old Italian saying goes: *"NADIA! WHADDYA MEAN YOU DROPPED OUT OF UNIVERSITY TO MAKE FUNNY VIDEOS?! WHEN I CATCH YOU I'M GONNA…" "… LEAVE ME ALONE, MOM! IT'S MY LIFE!!!"* … OK. Maybe it's not a "saying-saying" there…

servings: 4 to 6 | easy

GREEN CURRY SAUCE

In a food processor combine the basil, cilantro, lemongrass, green Thai chile, shallot, garlic, ginger, cumin, coriander, ¼ cup of coconut milk, lime juice, raw sugar, soy sauce, fish sauce, and black pepper, and blend into a paste.

Heat the canola oil in a large saucepan over medium-high heat and stir-fry the curry paste for a few minutes. Add the chicken stock and the kaffir lime leaves. Once boiling, turn down the heat to medium and simmer for 10 minutes.

SHKIAFFING IT TOGETHER

Slice the eggplant into ½-inch rounds, then into halves. To the simmering curry sauce add the eggplant, yellow pepper, and remaining coconut milk. Stir and cook for 15 to 20 minutes, until the vegetables are tender.

In a separate pot boil the udon noodles in salted water until al dente, then drain. Fill soup bowls with the hot udon noodles and smother with the spicy eggplant curry. If you like it hot, garnish with a red Thai chile.

GROCERY LIST

- ½ cup fresh basil leaves, packed
- ½ cup fresh cilantro leaves, packed
- 1 stalk lemongrass, chopped
- 1 green Thai chile, sliced
- 1 shallot, halved
- 2 garlic cloves, halved
- ½" knob fresh ginger, roughly chopped
- ½ tsp ground cumin
- ½ tsp ground coriander
- 1 cup coconut milk
- 1 lime, juiced
- 1 tsp raw sugar
- ¼ cup soy sauce
- 1 tbsp fish sauce
- freshly cracked black pepper, to taste
- 2 tbsp canola oil
- 3 cups chicken or vegetable stock
- 3 fresh kaffir lime leaves
- 1 eggplant
- 1 yellow bell pepper, sliced into ½"-wide strips
- 1 lb udon noodles
- red Thai chiles (optional)

GEAR

- food processor
- large saucepan
- large pot

"My family was too poor to afford fancy things like 'school' or 'pants.' So as a young man, I spent my days staring longingly at the Raanana College Campus, pained and pantless. The police eventually arrested me, but what I try to say is that you don't need fancy school to make it! All you need is passion, Wikipedia, and bail money."

bratwurst + pinto bean stew

I love pinto beans, the way they fizz and explode in your mouth… No, wait a minute, that's Pop Rocks, never mind.

servings: 4 to 6 | easy

SHKIAFFING IT TOGETHER

Heat a large saucepan over medium-high heat and sauté the bacon, onion, and sausage for 10 minutes, or until the onion and sausage start to brown. Add the carrots and celery, and sauté for 5 minutes. Deglaze the pan with ½ cup of beer, and reduce for 1 minute or until it's almost dry. Add the tomato paste, stir, and cook for 1 minute. Sprinkle in the all-purpose flour, stir to coat all the ingredients in the pan, and cook for 1 minute, stirring constantly. Add the stock, thyme, remaining beer, and pinto beans. Stir and simmer over medium-low heat for 15 minutes. Season with sea salt and freshly ground pepper to taste. Serve with crusty bread for dipping in the sauce.

GROCERY LIST
- 6 slices bacon, diced
- 1 yellow onion, diced
- 4 bratwurst sausages, sliced into ½" rounds
- 3 carrots, diced
- 3 celery ribs, diced
- 1½ cups honey brown beer
- 3 tbsp tomato paste
- ¼ cup all-purpose flour
- 2 cups beef stock
- ¼ tsp dried thyme
- 3 cups canned pinto beans, drained & rinsed
- sea salt & freshly ground black pepper, to taste

GEAR
- large saucepan

nadvice

Premade broths and canned beans are a life-saver when you're pressed for time. Just sauté your favorite vegetables, throw in some stock and beans, and *Tsaketa — a stew in no time. Experiment with spices for interesting variations.

pierogies w/ fixins

Pierogies are college comfort food at its best. Let me tell you a story… See, when I was a kid, I used to get real nervous about drawing princesses. Every time I put one on paper, I had to close my eyes and actively replenish the princess supply. I was scared that one day all the princesses would be gone, used up, and that I'd be left with… nothing. What?! I said I had a story, I didn't say I had a relevant story…On to our pierogies.

servings: 12 pierogies | intermediate

POTATO-CHEESE FILLING

Cook the potatoes and garlic in a large pot of boiling salted water until they're fork-tender, about 15 minutes. Strain. In a medium-sized bowl, mash together the potatoes and garlic, butter, heavy cream, green onions, cheddar cheese, red wine vinegar, ¼ teaspoon of sea salt, and freshly ground pepper to taste. Cover and set aside.

DOUGH

Add the flour to a large mixing bowl and make a well in the center. Into the well add the egg, milk, and ¼ teaspoon of sea salt. Using your hands, mix in the flour until all the liquid is absorbed and the dough sticks together. Shape the dough into a ball, wrap it in plastic wrap, and refrigerate for 20 minutes. Once the dough has chilled, dust a clean surface with flour, and roll it out ⅛ inch thick. Using the cookie cutter, cut out 12 circles.

PIEROGIES

On one half of each dough circle place 1 tablespoon of the potato mixture. Fold the other half of the circle over the potato mixture, and use a fork to press and seal the edges together. Lay out the pierogies on a large cookie sheet, and cover with a dish towel. In a medium pot, bring water to a boil, and drop in the pierogies 4 at a time. Boil uncovered for about 10 minutes, until they float to the surface. Strain.

SHKIAFFING IT TOGETHER

Mix the sour cream with the minced sweet gherkins and set aside. Heat the canola oil in a medium-sized pan over medium-high heat. Add the yellow onion slices, and fry until they're dark and crisp, 3 to 5 minutes. Drain. Discard all but 2 tablespoons of the oil, and pan-sear the pierogies in it for about 45 seconds per side, until they're lightly browned. Top the pierogies with the fried onion slivers and serve with the sweet gherkin sour cream.

GROCERY LIST

- 2 russet potatoes, cubed
- 2 garlic cloves
- 1 tsp unsalted butter
- ¼ cup heavy cream
- 2 green onions, thinly sliced
- ¼ cup grated aged cheddar
- 2 tsp red wine vinegar
- ½ tsp sea salt
- freshly ground black pepper, to taste
- 2 cups all-purpose flour
- 1 egg
- ½ cup whole milk
- ½ cup sour cream
- 6 sweet gherkins, minced
- canola oil, for deep-frying onions
- 1 small yellow onion, sliced ¼" thick

GEAR

- large pot
- medium mixing bowl
- large mixing bowl
- rolling pin
- 4" round cookie cutter
- large cookie sheet
- medium pot
- medium frying pan

When it comes to the filling, try a mixture of minced mushrooms and fried ground beef. Or whip up some sweet pierogies stuffed with mascarpone and berries. Honestly, it doesn't affect me.

no-bake cream cheese peanut butter pie

I have a great low-fat dessert that'll help you avoid the Freshman 15. But this isn't it. Nope, the lack of a dorm room oven gives us the perfect excuse to indulge in a no-bake cream cheese peanut butter pie! You're welcome.

servings: 8 | easy

PRETZEL CRUST

Put the salted pretzels in a food processor and pulse until fine. In a large bowl mix together the pretzel crumbs, ¼ cup of brown sugar, and the melted butter. Press the crust mixture into the pie plate. Refrigerate for 30 minutes.

CREAM CHEESE PEANUT BUTTER FILLING

In a medium bowl, combine the cream cheese, ¼ cup of brown sugar, and peanut butter, and whip until smooth using a hand mixer. In another medium bowl whip 1 cup of heavy cream with ¼ cup of brown sugar until stiff peaks form. Delicately fold the whipped cream into the cream cheese mixture. Spoon the filling into the pie shell and refrigerate for 1 hour.

CHOCOLATE WHIPPED CREAM

Heat 1 cup of heavy cream in a medium saucepan just until bubbles form around the edges; don't let it boil. Remove from the heat. Add the chopped chocolate, and whisk until melted. Refrigerate for 1 hour.

SHKIAFFING IT TOGETHER

Once the chocolate cream is cool, whip until thick. Slather the pie with the chocolate whipped cream, and garnish with the crushed peanuts (optional). Refrigerate for 3 hours to set.

GROCERY LIST

- 1¼ cups salted pretzels
- ¾ cup dark brown sugar
- ¼ cup unsalted butter, melted
- ½ cup cream cheese, at room temperature
- ⅓ cup smooth peanut butter
- 2 cups heavy cream
- 6 oz semi-sweet dark chocolate, finely chopped
- crushed peanuts (optional)

GEAR

- food processor
- 9" round pie plate
- 2 medium mixing bowls
- electric hand mixer
- medium saucepan

nadvice

Chin up, students! As tough as college may be, it's worth it! Eventually you'll graduate, proud, and realize that all that hard work gets you an unpaid internship at *Bitchin' Kitchen*. Whaddya gonna do.

veg-head extravaganza

*S*ure I poke fun at vegetarians, but between you and me — I eat vegetarian 80 percent of the time. Relax, I love meat. But I believe meat is a treat to be enjoyed occasionally — like cheesecake, or blackouts.

When I was a teen I became a vegetarian because "animals are people too." Back then I also thought *Braveheart* was a "deep" film, and a lizard tattoo meant something more than "I am a twit." Now I eat mostly vegetarian not for political reasons, but because it's healthy and affordable. Granted there's some cheap meat out there, but I'd rather get my protein from a hangnail than from 3 pounds of mystery beef for $3.99. On that note, let's debunk some vegetarian myths…

MYTH 1 Vegetarian meals lack protein. Folks, 1½ cups of chickpeas has more protein than a pork chop (and half the flavor, *cough*).

MYTH 2 Carbs make you fat. No, fat makes you fat, you *newrdz!

MYTH 3 Tofu sucks. …Yea, well, it's all about how you cook it. Besides, vegetarian dishes don't require tofu! That's like saying all meat dishes "require" filet mignon, or all food personalities "require" personality.

People have *all kinds of kooky theories on diet. Have you ever heard of the "Blood Type Diet" theory? It states that different blood types are genetically required to eat certain things, and for Type O's, meat is mandatory. I know this because one of my best friends is Type O. And after years of *shkoffing tons of meat, believe it or not, her cholesterol was surprisingly… that of *a 60-year-old truck driver*. Moral of the story: Don't believe what you wanna hear, and make some vegetarian recipes once in a while. Let's get cooking.

grilled apricot + feta salad

Sweet apricots grilled to juicy perfection, creamy feta cheese, pickled onions, and fresh mint, drizzled with a tangy champagne-poppy vinaigrette…

servings: 4 | easy

CHAMPAGNE-POPPY VINAIGRETTE

In a food processor, blend 4 tablespoons of extra-virgin olive oil, 3 tablespoons of champagne vinegar, honey, vanilla extract, and garlic clove. Fold in the poppy seeds, sea salt, and freshly ground pepper.

GRILLED APRICOTS

Heat a barbecue or a grill pan to medium-high. Baste the apricot halves with extra-virgin olive oil. Using tongs, sear the fleshy side of the apricots for 90 seconds, and then turn over to sear the skin side for 1 minute more. Remove them from the heat, and let cool.

PICKLED ONIONS

Heat a small saucepan over medium-high heat. Add the onion slices, pour in the remaining champagne vinegar, stir, and simmer until the onion slices turn bright pink, about 30 seconds. Remove from the heat and let cool slightly.

SHKIAFFING IT TOGETHER

Divide the apricot halves equally among 4 plates. Sprinkle each serving with ¼ cup of crumbled feta and a heaping tablespoon of pickled onions. Drizzle with the vinaigrette, and garnish with fresh mint leaves.

GROCERY LIST

- 6 tbsp extra-virgin olive oil
- ⅓ cup champagne vinegar
- 1 tbsp creamed honey
- 1 tsp vanilla extract
- ½ garlic clove
- 1 tbsp poppy seeds
- sea salt & freshly ground black pepper, to taste
- 8 apricots, halved & pitted
- ½ small red onion, finely sliced
- 1 cup crumbled feta cheese
- 4 fresh mint leaves

GEAR

- food processor
- barbecue or grill pan
- basting brush
- tongs
- small saucepan

gazpacho

I'm gonna be honest with you: when I first came across gazpacho, I didn't trust it. An uncooked soup was as foreign to me as an uncooked soup. But as with any minimalist recipe, it's the quality of the ingredients that makes all the difference. That being said, I'd go all organic with gazpacho, so you can really appreciate bright, fresh flavor of this delightful uncooked soup.

servings: 4 to 6 | easy

SHKIAFFING IT TOGETHER

In a large bowl whisk together the tomato juice, chilled vegetable broth, hot sauce, celery salt, and freshly ground pepper. Add all the diced veggies and the fresh dill, and stir to combine. Chill the gazpacho. Ladle into bowls and serve with your favorite crusty bread.

GROCERY LIST

- 3 cups tomato juice
- 1½ cups vegetable broth, chilled
- 1 tsp hot sauce
- ½ tsp celery salt
- freshly ground black pepper, to taste
- 1 green bell pepper, finely diced
- 1 red bell pepper, finely diced
- 1 orange bell pepper, finely diced
- 1 English cucumber, seeded & finely diced
- 1 bunch radishes, finely diced
- 1 red onion, finely diced
- 3 ripe tomatoes, finely diced
- ½ cup minced fresh dill

GEAR

- large mixing bowl

chana dhansak

The tamarind gives this unique curry a sweet kick, the creamy beans will have you *all worried about the lack of meat, and last but not least, you'll get some Indian culinary street cred for finally venturing beyond butter chicken or sag.

servings: 4 to 6 | easy

CURRY

Heat the ghee in a large saucepan over medium heat. Sauté the garlic, red chile, and ginger for 1 minute, until the garlic is golden. Add the red onion, and sauté it for 12 minutes until you get some golden, caramelized crispy bits. Then add the dhansak spice mix, stir, and sauté for 1 more minute to toast the spices.

Deglaze the saucepan with the vegetable stock. Add the tamarind paste, split red lentils, and sweet potato, stir, and simmer for 15 minutes. Remove the garlic and ginger pieces, then add the chickpeas (chana) and sea salt, and heat through for 5 minutes.

SHKIAFFING IT TOGETHER

Spoon the curry into a bowl, sprinkle with the cilantro, top it off with some crispy fried onion slivers, and serve with brown rice, naan, or a whole-wheat pita.

GROCERY LIST
- ¼ cup ghee (see page 32)
- 2 garlic cloves, smashed
- 1 fresh red chile pepper, minced
- 1" knob fresh ginger
- 1 red onion, diced
- 1 batch Dhansak Spice Blend, ground (see page 33)
- 4 cups vegetable stock
- 2 tbsp tamarind paste
- ¾ cup dried split red lentils
- 1 sweet potato, diced
- 3 cups canned chickpeas, drained
- ¼ tsp sea salt
- ¼ cup minced fresh cilantro
- fried onion slivers (see page 21)
- brown rice, naan, or whole-wheat pita

GEAR
- large saucepan

"May I suggest some plump, juicy chicken in dat Dhansak... I know. I know. Dis is a 'vegetarian' chapter, but it's all how you look at tings! Dey say you are what you eat, right? Well chickens eat grain...so wouldn't dat make chicken: A GRAIN?"

ghee

Ghee is basically clarified brown butter. What the French consider a delicacy, the Indians cook with every day — how awesome is that?! Ghee not only adds a rich and nutty flavor to your dishes, but it also has a shelf life of a year unrefrigerated!

GROCERY LIST
- 1¼ cups unsalted butter

GEAR
- medium saucepan
- cheesecloth
- sieve or fine-mesh strainer

servings: 1 cup | easy

SHKIAFFING IT TOGETHER

Simmer the butter in a medium-sized saucepan over medium-low heat for 10 to 15 minutes. Whatever you do, never stir ghee, just delicately skim off the froth. You know it's done when you see some golden brown protein bits at the bottom and the butter begins to turn an amber color. The second it starts to turn amber, take it off the heat immediately or you'll burn the ghee. Let it cool for about 30 minutes; then strain it through cheesecloth into a jar.

dhansak spice blend

Now to make a dhansak, you need a dhansak spice blend, so let's toast some spices. And when I say "some" I mean "a f@#k-load." You ready for this?

servings: 1 portion of spice blend | easy

SHKIAFFING IT TOGETHER

Heat a medium-sized pan over medium-high heat. Add the spices, and toast them for a few minutes, until fragrant. Stir the spices continuously, being careful not to burn them. Once the spices are toasted, remove the spice mix from the pan immediately, and store it in a jar with a tight-fitting lid.

GROCERY LIST
- ½ tsp cumin seeds
- ½ tsp fennel seeds
- ½ tsp coriander seeds
- ½ tsp cardamom seeds
- ½ tsp sesame seeds
- ½ tsp peppercorns
- ½ tsp ground turmeric
- 3 cloves
- ¼ tsp ground nutmeg
- ¼ tsp ground cinnamon
- ½ tsp fenugreek seeds

GEAR
- medium pan
- glass jar with a tight-fitting lid

"There are so many spices mentioned in this recipe, I almost had to call my agent! . . . Then I realized that he doesn't exist. Now most of these spices you are familiar with, so let's focus on the most exotic — fenugreek. This is both an herb and a spice: the fenugreek leaves are spinachlike and bitter, but the seeds taste like maple syrup! It's true! They taste so much like maple syrup that they are the main ingredient in artificial maple syrup! Here is some thought for food: Fenugreek originated in the Middle East. How strange is it that in a land without sugar maple trees, a maple syrup flavor exists within the fenugreek seed?! It almost makes you wonder, is there a beautiful Yeheskel somewhere in Alabama? . . . Where are you?"

buckwheat raclette – gluten-free

I'll never forget the first time I tried a gluten-free cookie. I bit into it and said to myself: "Oh, so that's what gluten is… the stuff that makes a cookie good." Just kidding, I didn't say anything, I just spit it out. But a lot of people have gluten allergies these days, so we're gonna cook up a delicious recipe that's *naturally* gluten-free: buckwheat pancakes topped with tender new potatoes, smothered in a raclette cheese sauce and maple syrup!

servings: 4 | intermediate

POTATOES

Cook the potatoes in a large pot of boiling salted water for 15 minutes, until tender. Drain and cut them in half.

BUCKWHEAT PANCAKES

In a large bowl combine the buckwheat flour, milk, water, egg, and sea salt, and whisk until the batter is smooth. Cover it, and let it rest on the counter for 30 minutes. Once the batter has rested, heat the butter in a nonstick pan over medium heat. Pour in silver dollars of batter, about ¼ cup per pancake. When the top of a pancake has little bubbles in it, gently turn it over and cook for about 2 more minutes. You want them to be golden and lightly browned on both sides.

RACLETTE SAUCE

Heat the half-and-half in a small pot over medium-low heat. When the cream starts to steam, don't let it boil; take it off the heat. Immediately add the raclette cheese and freshly cracked pepper. Turn the heat down to low, place the pot back on the burner, and stir continuously until the cheese has melted into a creamy sauce. Cover and keep warm.

SHKIAFFING IT TOGETHER

Place a few pancakes on a big plate. Add ½ cup of new potatoes, and ladle on ¼ cup of the raclette cheese sauce. Drizzle with maple syrup, and serve with a couple of sweet gherkins on the side.

GROCERY LIST

- *2 cups bite-sized new potatoes*
- *1 cup buckwheat flour*
- *1 cup whole milk*
- *½ cup water*
- *1 egg*
- *¼ tsp sea salt*
- *1 tbsp unsalted butter*
- *1 cup half & half*
- *¾ cup finely grated raclette cheese*
- *¼ tsp freshly cracked black pepper*
- *2 tbsp maple syrup*
- *1 jar sweet gherkins*

GEAR

- *large pot*
- *large mixing bowl*
- *large nonstick pan*
- *small pot*

POTATO
ARE
PEOPLE Too

"May I tempt you with some Iberian ham, bro? Just imagine: savory ham smothered in dat creamy cheese sauce and sweet maple syrup… I know, 'vegetarian, vegetarian.' But you tink those potatoes didn't suffer?! Bruised and alone in a dark pantry with nothing to do but wait for death: Skinned alive! Boiled! Thrown into scalding hot oil! Shame on you, *bro. Shame on you."

vegan dark chocolate + caramelized banana pie

Everybody pokes fun at vegans, but in their defense, they're the only humans who aren't sucking on a cow teat at 40. On that note, we're making a *"you-wouldn't-even-know-it's-vegan"* Dark Chocolate & Caramelized Banana Pie.

servings: 6 | easy

COCONUT ALMOND CRUST

Preheat the oven to 300°F. In a large bowl combine the sweetened coconut, almonds, ¼ cup of melted cocoa butter, vanilla extract, and sea salt, and mix until combined and crumbly. Grease a springform pan with 1 tablespoon of cocoa butter. Mold the crust mixture into it, pushing it up along the sides. Bake it for 20 to 25 minutes, or until the coconut is lightly browned. Remove it from the oven and let it cool.

DARK CHOCOLATE FILLING

Melt the dark chocolate in the top pan of a double boiler over medium heat, stirring until creamy. Once it has melted, remove it from the heat and let it cool down for about 10 minutes. In a large bowl combine the silken tofu, soy milk, maple syrup, and the cooled melted dark chocolate, and blend with a hand mixer on high speed for 10 minutes, or until completely smooth. This mixture should have a pudding-like texture.

CARAMELIZED BANANAS

Preheat the oven to 250°F. Generously coat the sliced bananas in raw sugar. Place them in an even layer on a baking sheet that is covered with parchment paper. Bake for 15 to 20 minutes or until caramelized. Let cool.

SHKIAFFING IT TOGETHER

Pour the dark chocolate filling into the piecrust and chill for 2 hours. Top the pie with a layer of caramelized bananas, starting from the middle and working your way outwards in a spiral. Chill it for another 30 minutes to set.

GROCERY LIST
- 1 cup sweetened shredded coconut
- ¼ cup pulverized almonds
- ¼ cup + 1 tbsp cocoa butter, melted
- ¼ tsp natural vanilla extract
- ¼ tsp sea salt
- 1 cup finely chopped dark chocolate
- 1 cup silken tofu
- 2 tbsp soy milk
- 1 tbsp maple syrup
- 3 bananas, sliced into ¼" rounds
- raw sugar

GEAR
- 2 large mixing bowls
- 9" springform pan
- double boiler
- electric hand mixer
- baking sheet
- parchment paper

Nadventure

Cocoa butter is the fat derived from cocoa beans — the stuff that makes chocolate creamy. It's a great dairy-free replacement for butter. Also, cocoa butter doesn't raise cholesterol levels like butter does, so whether you're vegan or not, try swapping it out in your recipes. You can find cocoa butter in natural/organic food stores. It's a staple of vegan baking.

bitchin' booty camp XTREME

*H*ave you ever sat there late at night watching workout infomercials, feeling bloated, sweaty, and enraged? If so, you should really talk to someone. But if you wanna drop a few pounds to rock some slutty jeggings, you've come to the right place!

That's right, America! In this chapter we're gonna pummel your muffin tops, throttle your beer gut, and bite you right in the cankle. Listen up, because it's time to whip your *musholite body into shape with our Bitchin' Booty Camp *XTREME!*

Let's face it, I'm ripped. But it wasn't always this way…one glass of wine used to cut it. Bah. Here are the pillars to getting into Bitchin' shape:

MEASURE YOUR FATS There're 14 grams of fat in 1 tablespoon of olive oil — that's half the fat found in a freakin' burger! A drizzle here, a drizzle there, and before you know it you've *shkoffed a day's worth of fat and you haven't even chewed any solids yet! Whatever you do, *DON'T EYEBALL IT.*

NEVER SKIP MEALS As the old Italian saying goes: "A shake for breakfast, a shake for lunch, and your thighs still shake for dinner." Skipping meals makes your body think it's starving, so it holds on to fat for dear life, literally. Always eat three to five logically portioned meals a day to keep your metabolism up.

ONLY BUY FRESH INGREDIENTS I can hear some people whining already: *"But fresh ingredients are expensive!!!"* Umm, no. Processed ingredients are expensive, check yourself. Ugh, now I can hear others complaining: *"Goddamit! The freakin' car battery is dead!"* Never mind, that was just some random dude outside.

EXERCISE The hardest part of getting into shape is staying motivated to exercise, *arck!* And that's why I have a personal trainer; I'm too lazy to even cancel appointments. What? Don't look at me like that — trainers can be cheap! You can find a fitness student on Craigslist who's willing to work your booty for $20 an hour. You can also find personal trainers.

It's not about being skinny, it's about feeling good in your skin. These recipes will definitely turbocharge your fitness regimen, but know that just cooking from scratch is a huge step in the right direction. So let's get cooking.

turkey cassoulet w/ butter beans

Now cassoulet usually has some pancetta or sausage for a smoky salty kick… It also usually has some goose, duck, and totally different beans. Pfft. Technicalities.

servings: 4 | easy

SHKIAFFING IT TOGETHER

Preheat the oven to 325°F. Heat the canola oil in a large nonstick pan over medium-high heat. Massage the turkey drumsticks with the smoked paprika, pepper, and sea salt. Pan-sear them for a few minutes on all sides until golden and crispy. In a roasting pan combine the chicken stock, San Marzano tomatoes, maple syrup, onions, garlic, thyme, parsley, bay leaf, and butter beans, and mix well. Add the pan-seared turkey drumsticks on top, cover, and cook in the oven for 2 hours.

Spoon the cassoulet into a bowl, garnish with fresh parsley, and serve with whole-grain bread for dipping.

GROCERY LIST

- 2 tbsp canola oil
- 4 turkey drumsticks (or more)
- 1 tbsp smoked paprika
- ½ tsp freshly cracked black pepper
- ¼ tsp sea salt
- 4 cups low-sodium chicken stock
- 2 cups canned San Marzano plum tomatoes, hand-crushed
- 2 tbsp maple syrup
- 2 yellow onions, sliced into ½"-thick rounds
- 2 garlic cloves, crushed
- 1 fresh thyme sprig
- ¼ cup flat-leaf parsley, minced, + extra for garnish
- 1 bay leaf
- ½ lb dried butter beans, rinsed

GEAR

- large nonstick pan
- roasting pan

"Turkey can be a dry bird, bro, but not da legs! Dat dark meat is juicy, tender, and only 13 grams of fat per leg. Not bad, not bad at all. Did you know dat certain extinct species of turkey date as far back as 23 million years ago? …Which makes no sense bro, because everybody knows dat God created da earth 10,000 years ago! So dis must mean one of two tings: turkeys are aliens, or turkeys created God."

egg white, caramelized onion + fig jam sandwich

I eat this sandwich a coupla times a week — it's so good that you wouldn't even know it's diet food. See, caramelized onions are king when you're dieting: they're super low in fat, super cheap, and make anything taste great (…well, anything that tastes great with caramelized onions).

servings: 4 | easy

CARAMELIZED ONIONS

Heat 1 tablespoon of extra-virgin olive oil in a large nonstick frying pan over medium heat. Add the onions and ¼ teaspoon of sea salt, and stir to coat evenly. Sauté for 8 minutes. Then turn the heat down to medium-low and sauté for another 40 minutes, until they're a deep amber color and have reduced to one third of their original volume.

EGG WHITE OMELETS

Heat a medium nonstick pan over medium heat. Add a teaspoon of extra-virgin olive oil, and use a paper towel to lightly grease the pan and remove the excess oil. Beat 2 egg whites with ¼ teaspoon of piment d'Espelette, ¼ teaspoon of sea salt, and some freshly cracked black pepper. Pour the egg whites into the pan, and cook for about 3 minutes, until opaque and slightly firm. Flip over the egg white omelet, and cook for an additional minute or two. Repeat with the remaining eggs.

BLUEBERRY & ARUGULA SALAD

In a jar, combine 1 tablespoon of extra-virgin olive oil, aged balsamic, and maple syrup. Close the jar tightly and shake vigorously to emulsify. In a large bowl, toss the arugula and blueberries with the dressing.

SHKIAFFING IT TOGETHER

Toast the bread and slather one half of each sandwich with a tablespoon of fig jam and a tablespoon of caramelized onions. Add an egg white omelet, top with a second slice of toasted bread, and serve with 1 cup of arugula and blueberry salad on the side.

GROCERY LIST
- 2 tbsp + 1 tsp extra-virgin olive oil
- 3 red onions, sliced into ¼"-rings and separated
- 1¼ tsp sea salt
- 8 egg whites (2 egg whites per sandwich)
- 1 tsp piment d'Espelette
- freshly cracked black pepper, to taste
- 1 tbsp aged balsamic vinegar, minimum 7 years old
- 1 tbsp maple syrup
- 4 cups baby arugula
- 1 cup fresh blueberries
- 8 slices flax-seed or whole-wheat bread, sliced ½" thick
- fig jam (see page 47)

GEAR
- large nonstick frying pan
- medium nonstick frying pan
- small glass jar with tight-fitting lid
- large mixing bowl

nadvice

Most of the time we stuff our faces outta sheer boredom. So get a hobby! I find spending time reading a good book, or blinging-out a pair of heels with crystals, really lends itself to great eating habits (and even greater shoes).

creamy cream-less soups

All hail the humble potato! The addition of potato puree to soups gives you that creamy texture you're looking for without the fat.

servings: 4 to 6 | easy

CREAMY SOUP BASE

Heat the extra-virgin olive oil in a large soup pot over medium heat. Sauté the leeks for 5 minutes, until soft. Deglaze with the chicken stock, stir, and bring it to a simmer. Add the russet potatoes and cook for 15 minutes, until they are fork-tender.

CARROT-GINGER

Add the carrots and ginger at the same time as the potatoes. Cook for 15 minutes, until the carrots and potatoes are fork-tender.

SPINACH

Add the spinach in the last 5 minutes of cooking the potatoes. Once pureed, garnish with lemon slices.

TOMATO-PEPPER

Add the cherry tomatoes and red bell peppers at the same time as the potatoes. Cook for 15 minutes, until the peppers and potatoes are fork-tender. Once pureed, garnish with a big pinch of minced fresh dill.

SHKIAFFING IT TOGETHER

Add the maple syrup to your variation of the soup, and use a hand blender to puree it. Season it with sea salt and freshly ground pepper. You can add cooked whole-grain rice or small whole-grain pasta as well.

GROCERY LIST
- 1 tbsp extra-virgin olive oil
- 2 leeks, sliced into ¼" rounds
- 5 cups low-sodium chicken stock
- 2 large russet potatoes, diced

- 6 carrots, sliced into ¼" rounds
- 1 1" knob fresh ginger, minced OR

- 4 cups fresh spinach
- 1 lemon, sliced OR

- 2 cups cherry tomatoes, halved
- 2 red bell peppers, chopped
- fresh dill, for garnish

- 1 tbsp maple syrup
- sea salt & freshly ground black pepper, to taste

GEAR
- large soup pot
- immersion blender

"People always ask me, 'Hans, how do you get so buff?' Sure, I exercise like a beast and my great-grandfather was a centaur... but getting ripped is 80% diet! Simple rules: cut the fat, sugar, and sodium. Consume no more than 1 tablespoon of oil a day, 1 teaspoon of salt and sugar, and no processed foods whatsoever. Save the grease for where it belongs — on your chiseled chest."

rustic low-sugar jam

You can use this recipe for jam with any fruit. Mind that some fruits take longer than others to get saucy. For example, berries, figs, and fruits with no pit take about 30 to 40 minutes to cook into rustic jam. Stone fruits like apricots or plums may take an hour or more. Just keep an eye on it. As the old Italian saying goes, "It ain't rocket surgery."

GROCERY LIST
- ¼ cup water
- 1 pound fresh fruit, quartered
- ¼ cup raw sugar
- 1 tbsp grated lemon zest

GEAR
- medium saucepan

servings: 1 cup of jam | easy

SHKIAFFING IT TOGETHER

In a medium saucepan, bring the water to a simmer over medium heat. Once the water is simmering, turn the heat down to low and add the fruit, sugar, and lemon zest. Stir and simmer uncovered for 30 minutes (or up to an hour or more, depending on the type of fruit you used). Stir often until it's thick and syrupy, but note that this low-sugar jam won't have a jelly-like consistency like store-bought jam; it'll be looser and more rustic.

stone fruit en papillote w/ nonfat vanilla-infused yogurt

Nonfat yogurt is a great blank-canvas dessert. Enjoy it with a shot of chilled espresso and an ounce of shaved dark chocolate, or get fancy and *shkoff it with fruit en papillote…

servings: 4 | easy

MARINADE

In a small saucepan, bring the water to a simmer over medium heat. Add the vanilla bean pod, 2 tablespoons of honey, star anise, and lime zest, and simmer for 2 to 3 minutes, until reduced by half. Add the fresh lime juice, stir, and set aside.

VANILLA YOGURT

In a medium-sized bowl whisk together the yogurt, vanilla bean seeds, and 1 tablespoon of honey. Let the mixture sit, covered, at room temperature until the fruit is ready.

SHKIAFFING IT TOGETHER

Preheat the oven to 400°F, and position a rack in the center of the oven. Place a large piece of parchment paper on a baking sheet. Place all the fruit in a single layer on the center of the parchment paper, and pour the marinade over the fruit. Fold the parchment over the ingredients, making small overlapping folds to seal the edges tight (this parchment sack is called a "papillote"). Bake for 15 minutes or until you can see the juices bubbling. Remove from the oven, and open the parchment to let the fruit cool slightly. Discard the lime zest and vanilla bean pod. Divide the fruit among 4 plates, and drizzle each portion with any liquid that remains in the parchment paper. Garnish each plate with a generous dollop of vanilla yogurt and sprinkle with ½ teaspoon of maple sugar (optional).

GROCERY LIST

- ¼ cup water
- ½ vanilla bean, seeds separated from pod
- 3 tbsp honey
- 1 star anise pod
- 1" strip lime zest
- 1 tbsp fresh lime juice
- 1 cup Greek or Mediterranean non-fat yogurt
- 2 plums, pitted & quartered
- 1 cup sweet or sour cherries, pitted
- 1 peach, pitted & quartered
- 2 apricots, pitted & quartered
- 2 tsp maple sugar (optional)

GEAR

- small saucepan
- medium mixing bowl
- parchment paper
- baking sheet

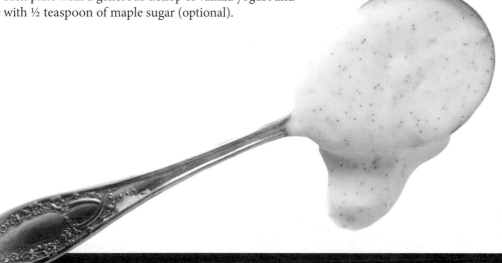

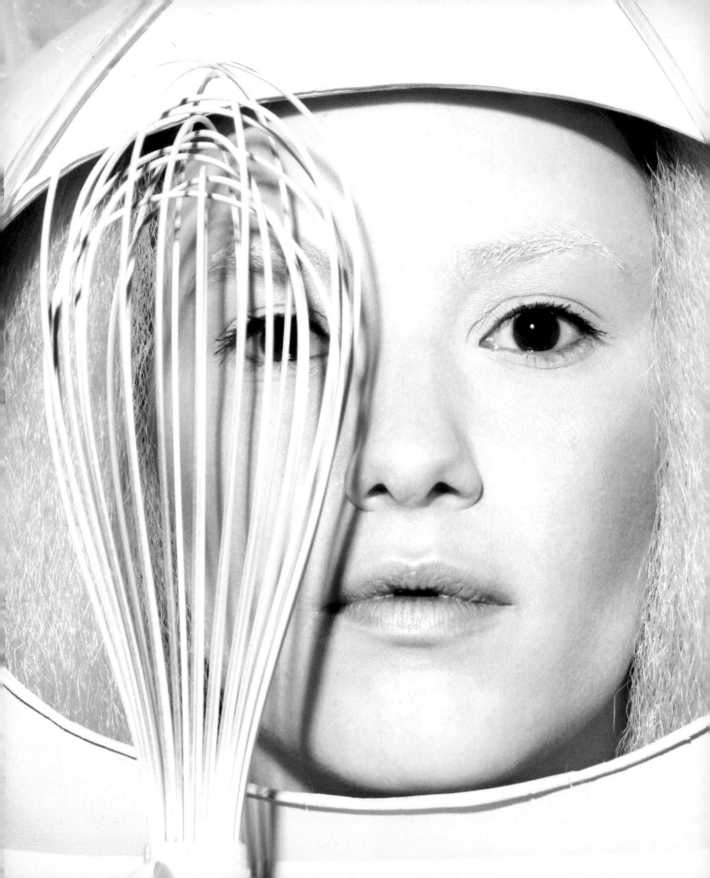

hi-speed suppers

The internet rocks. But as much as you love the Web, sometimes you need to step away from the computer and cook a good meal…in under 30 minutes so you can get back to surfing, *stat!*

*Bey yea. I'll be the first to admit that I spend most of my time online, and I can't imagine life without it: You have a question, *Tsakcta, you find the answer; You wanna start a business, *Tsaketa*, you build a site (and fail). Man, the Web has gotten so freakin' advanced, you don't even need to spell anymore! Just smash your hand down on the keyboard, and Google's like: *Did you mean: Topless photos of Christian Bale?*…Look, sometimes Google is wrong there, but, uh, you get the picture.

Yet despite all of these epic advancements, some geezers still have the gall to complain that *"the Web is pushing us further apart!"*…And that's a bad thing? I don't know about you, but human contact makes me uncomfortable — all those germs and awkward silences…To go out and party like a savage, that's one thing. But to trek all the way to a neon-lit coffee shop so I can exchange the in-person equivalent of three emoticons, *ma get outta here! Whatever you have to say, 140 characters is sufficient. Unless, as I mentioned earlier, it's time to party like a savage.

So in honor of the freedoms bestowed upon us by the digital age, we're gonna cook up some quick dishes you can *shkoff one-handed. This way you can get back to the important things, like stalking your high-school enemies on Facebook. (Marco, Vanessa, I'm watching you.)

L3t'5 g3t c00k1ng.

The Top 3 Things You Need to Stop Doing on Facebook

3) Tagging people in useless calendars designed by the color-blind. Oh wow, your birthday is on June 4th, and mine is on May 12th! Riveting.

2) Forgetting to assess your demographic. Sorry Bob, I won't be able to attend your "Vegan Vampire Bubble Tea Party" — I have other, less enraging plans.

1) Playing nerdy games in public. Seriously, if you've reached such a low that you're hunting for "magical eggs" to build a "happy shed," do yourself a favor and at least pretend to look busy.

saltimbocca veal cutlet sandwich

Cutlet sandwiches are the best! I love them so much that I actually stole one from a classmate in fifth grade. Seriously. This kid always had big paninis full of the good stuff. So I memorized his locker combination, sneaked outta class, broke into his locker, and stole his cutlet sandwich. If that doesn't scream Italian, I don't know what does.

servings: 4 | easy

CUTLETS

Using a meat mallet, pound the veal cutlets ¼ inch thick. Then dip the veal cutlets in the beaten eggs, and coat them with the Italian seasoned breadcrumbs. In a large frying pan, heat the canola oil to 350°F, and fry the cutlets for 2 to 3 minutes per side, until golden, crispy, and cooked through. Drain the cutlets on paper towels. Add the prosciutto slices to the pan, and fry for about 1 minute, until very crispy. Drain the crispy prosciutto on paper towels.

SAGE MAYO

In a small bowl mix the mayonnaise with the sweet gherkins and sage.

SHKIAFFING IT TOGETHER

Slather each kaiser roll with sage mayonnaise, add a cutlet and a slice of crispy prosciutto, and top it off with some baby romaine leaves.

GROCERY LIST
- 4 cutlets free-raised veal
- 3 eggs, beaten
- 1 cup Italian seasoned breadcrumbs
- 1/4 cup canola oil
- 4 slices prosciutto di Parma
- ½ cup mayonnaise
- 3 sweet gherkins, minced
- 1 tbsp minced fresh sage
- 4 kaiser rolls, halved and toasted
- 10 fresh baby romaine leaves

GEAR
- meat mallet
- large frying pan
- small mixing bowl

"Veal is a touchy subject, *bro. But what's nice about 'free-raised' veal is that the calves are free to roam the open pastures with their mothers, snuggling and prancing. They may not live a long life, but at least it's a good life. Anyways, if you don't wanna use veal for whatever reason — like maybe you're a compassionate human being with a conscience and a soul — you can always go with beef tenderloin or chicken breast, sliced thin and pounded."

spicy shrimp po boy

Sometimes I get what I like to call "emotional Tourette's." Like, a friend will casually mention that they took a nice walk today, and I'll respond, "Nice, I love walks…" but in a totally abrupt and inappropriate tone, the same tone you'd use if you had to say "You bastard, you killed my sea monkeys!" Weird.

servings: 4 | easy

SPICY REMOULADE SAUCE

In a food processor puree the mayonnaise, horseradish, garlic, habañero, lime juice, and parsley.

SHRIMP

In a medium-sized bowl whisk together the eggs and milk. In another bowl mix together the flour, cayenne, salt, and pepper. Preheat the oven to 400°F. In a medium-sized skillet or saucepan heat the canola oil over medium-high heat. Dip a shrimp in the egg mixture, then dredge in the flour mixture. Fry 6 to 8 shrimp at a time for about 3 minutes, turning the shrimp once. Remove the shrimp from the pan with a slotted spoon, and drain on paper towels. Repeat with the remaining shrimp.

SHKIAFFING IT TOGETHER

Warm the Greek pitas in the oven for 1 or 2 minutes. Slather the pitas generously with the spicy remoulade sauce. Add a small handful of baby arugula. Top with 6 shrimp and sprinkle with cherry tomatoes.

GROCERY LIST

- 1 cup mayonnaise
- 1 tbsp prepared horseradish
- 2 garlic cloves
- ½ habañero chile, roughly chopped
- 1 lime, juiced
- ¼ cup flat-leaf parsley leaves
- 2 eggs
- ½ cup whole milk
- ½ cup all-purpose flour
- ½ tsp cayenne pepper
- ½ tsp sea salt
- freshly ground black pepper, to taste
- 2 tbsp canola or peanut oil
- 24 large shrimp, shelled & deveined
- 4 6" soft Greek pitas
- 2 cups baby arugula
- 2 cups cherry or grape tomatoes, halved

GEAR

- food processor
- 2 medium mixing bowls
- medium skillet
- slotted spoon

nadvice

The definition of a virus is "a living entity that uses a host to reproduce and survive." Every second that we spend online, we're helping the Web replicate — bit by bit, byte by byte. So it begs the question: Are we using the Web, or is the Web using us? Has humanity become a slave host to a digital virus hell-bent on expansion? As we spend more time online working, playing, socializing, are we "Net-Gen," or just feeding the beast? What does it matter?! You can't turn it off, from banking to medical, we now need IT to survive. . . . Gotta go. Feeding time.

aged cheddar cauliflower soup

This creamy cauliflower soup is kinda like the nerdy chick who magically becomes hot once she takes off her glasses and slaps on a pancetta dress.

servings: 4 to 6 | easy

PANCETTA

In a large pot, heat the extra-virgin olive oil over medium heat. Add the diced pancetta and sauté it for a few minutes, until crispy. Remove the pancetta from the pot using a slotted spoon and drain on paper towels.

SOUP

In the pancetta oil, sauté the leeks for a few minutes, until soft. Deglaze the pot with the chicken stock. Add the cauliflower, russets, and bay leaf to the stock and simmer for 15 minutes, until the veggies are fork-tender. Remove the pot from the heat. Fish out about 1 cup of cauliflower florets and potatoes, and set them aside.

SHKIAFFING IT TOGETHER

Puree the soup using a hand blender, and then put the cauliflower and potatoes pieces back into the pot. Add the aged cheddar, sea salt, and freshly cracked pepper. Turn the heat down to medium-low and whisk for a few minutes, until the cheese is melted. Serve topped with the crispy pancetta and minced chives.

GROCERY LIST

- 1 tbsp extra-virgin olive oil
- 6 slices pancetta, finely diced
- 1 leek, thinly sliced
- 6 cups chicken stock
- 1 small cauliflower, chopped into bite-sized pieces
- 2 russet potatoes, diced
- 1 bay leaf
- ¾ cup finely grated aged cheddar cheese
- sea salt & freshly cracked black pepper, to taste
- minced fresh chives

GEAR

- large pot
- slotted spoon
- immersion blender

moroccan fig + butternut squash couscous

This sweet and savory Moroccan couscous is loaded with butternut squash, figs, and roasted pistachios. Sound good? Oh it is, it is.

servings: 6 | easy

MOROCCAN STEW

Heat the extra-virgin olive oil in a large saucepan over medium heat. Add the onions, garlic, cumin, turmeric, and cinnamon. Sauté for 2 to 3 minutes, until fragrant. Add the turnip, and sauté for 5 minutes. Deglaze with the chicken stock, and add the dried apricots, figs, zucchini, squash, red bell pepper, and chickpeas. Stir and simmer for about 15 minutes, until the veggies are tender. Discard the garlic, and add sea salt and freshly ground pepper to taste.

COUSCOUS

Put the couscous in a large bowl. Boil the water, and pour the boiling water over the couscous. Cover the bowl, and let it sit for about 5 minutes. Then fluff the couscous with a fork.

SHKIAFFING IT TOGETHER

Add ½ cup of couscous to each bowl, and ladle on the stew. Garnish with crushed roasted pistachios and minced cilantro.

GROCERY LIST

- 2 tbsp extra-virgin olive oil
- 2 yellow onions, diced
- 2 garlic cloves, smashed
- 1 tsp ground cumin
- 1 tsp ground turmeric
- ½ tsp ground cinnamon
- 1 turnip, cubed
- 4 cups chicken stock
- ½ cup dried apricots, quartered
- ½ cup dried figs, quartered
- 1 zucchini, cubed
- 1 butternut squash, cubed
- 1 red bell pepper, cubed
- 2 cups canned chickpeas, drained & rinsed
- sea salt & freshly ground black pepper, to taste
- 2 cups couscous
- 2½ cups water
- ½ cup roasted pistachios, crushed
- ⅓ cup fresh cilantro, minced

GEAR

- large saucepan
- large bowl

"I am so exciting about this Middle Eastern specialty — couscous! In Raanana couscous is the most popular! Almost as popular as the great SAMANTHA FOX!!! What makes this dish unique is the cinnamon. Whenever you taste something really delicious and wonder "what is that special flavor?," it is usually ketchup. But back to the cinnamon. Now, North Americans think cinnamon is for dessert only, but let me tell you, it is fantastical in savory dishes. Just remember to use little, because cinnamon can quickly dominate. And no one likes to be dominated by cinnamon. Cumin maybe — as long as it's wearing the real latex and not chintzy PVC imitation — but never cinnamon."

turkey time

Pssst! I'm going to let you in on a little secret… I have a turkey fetish. That's right, I don't just love turkey, I covet it. I grew up in an Italian family, man, we never had turkey! As a kid I chalked up our turkey-less existence to child abuse. The TV would mock me: polite well-dressed families sitting around the table, chuckling as they passed around that mysterious golden bird filled with something called "stuffing" and hope. Then I'd think of my family: yelling over each other with bits of ravioli stuck to their greasy chins, a bunch of cologne-drenched barbarians howling and cackling as they sucked back jugs of homemade wine and cut the cheese in more ways than one.

In the name of civilization, I pleaded with my mother, *"Please Ma! Please make some turkey!"* And she'd look at me like I'd suggested we roast the cat. "Nadia, Italians don't eat turkey." My little beady eyes squinted with spite, and I vowed right then and there that one day that turkey, and all the promise it held, would be mine. (Well, I didn't really "vow" vow, but I definitely went outside to torture some ants, same difference.)

These days I treat myself to turkey whenever I feel like it. It doesn't have to be a holiday. In fact it doesn't even have to be dinner. The mere presence of a turkey soothes me. But after cooking a coupla birds, I started to understand why my family nixed it altogether. I mean, plainly put, turkey can be a pain in the ass: Not only is it expensive, but all that defrosting, waiting, basting, stressing, break-dancing… It's too much!

But, if one turkey can be turned into a week's worth of meals, aha! It starts to add up. In fact, you almost *save* time and money. I apply this kind of creative math to my exorbitant shopping sprees as well. Just take the price of the item, divide it by how often you'll wear it, and for a mere dollar a day — less than the cost of feeding a starving child — you can own a pair of Louboutins.

Let's get cooking.

da bird

Behold the turkey! Now attack it with your face.

servings: 10 to 12 | easy

BUTTER

Heat a small saucepan over medium heat. Add the unsalted butter and simmer until the water in the butter has evaporated and the milk solids have either risen to the top or sunk to the bottom. Skim off the solids, and set the clarified butter aside.

TURKEY

Holding it over the sink, remove the bird from its packaging and discard the giblets (or use them for some other recipe…that you won't find in this cookbook). Rinse the bird inside and out with cold water, and pat it dry. Place the bird breast side up on the rack of a roasting pan. Tuck the wing tips under the body. Place the onions, sage, oregano, and bay leaves in the cavity. Seal both ends of the bird with skewers. Bring the legs together and tie them with cooking twine. Baste the bird with the clarified butter and sprinkle it generously with sea salt and freshly cracked pepper.

SHKIAFFING IT TOGETHER

Preheat the oven to 375°F. Cook the bird for 40 minutes, and then lower the temperature to 325°F. Without removing the bird from the oven, baste the bird with the clarified butter every 30 minutes during the entire length of cooking. If you find that the bird is getting too dark too early, tent it loosely with aluminum foil, but be sure to remove the foil for the last half hour if the skin needs more darkening. The bird is done when an instant-read thermometer reads 175°F when inserted into the meaty area of a thigh. Avoid the bone as it will give a false reading. Do your first temperature check after a little less than 3 hours of cooking. A 12- to 16-pound unstuffed turkey should take between 3¼ and 3½ hours to cook. Let the turkey sit for 20 minutes before carving so that the juices can redistribute.

GROCERY LIST
- ½ cup unsalted butter
- 1 12-to16-lb turkey, thawed if frozen
- 3 yellow onions, quartered
- 3 fresh sage sprigs
- 3 fresh oregano sprigs
- 3 bay leaves
- sea salt & freshly cracked black pepper

GEAR
- small saucepan
- large roasting pan with rack insert
- skewers
- kitchen twine
- basting brush
- instant-read thermometer

pancetta chestnut stuffing

Between you and me, stuffing may just be the real reason I love turkey. It's hard to tell — they're too closely associated in my mind. Its kinda like loving Nirvana and then being sucked into the Foo Fighters. Naw, not really…turkey definitely has more flavor than the Foo Fighters. *Go stuffing!*

servings: 4 to 6 | easy

BREADCUBES

Preheat the oven to 400°F. Scatter the bread cubes in a single layer on 2 large baking sheets, and oven-toast for about 15 minutes, until golden brown.

PANCETTA MIXTURE

Heat a large frying pan over medium heat, add the diced pancetta, and render it for couple of minutes, until crispy. Add the unsalted butter, onions, celery, sea salt, and freshly ground pepper. Stir, and sauté until the veggies have softened, about 10 minutes.

SHKIAFFING IT TOGETHER

In a large bowl whisk the chicken stock with the eggs. Add the toasted bread cubes, pancetta mixture, halved chestnuts, raisins, diced apricots, tarragon, and thyme. Mix thoroughly. Place the stuffing into a baking dish (or two), cover with foil, and bake for 40 minutes.

GROCERY LIST

- 4 cups cubed sourdough bread
- ½ cup finely diced pancetta
- ⅓ cup unsalted butter, melted
- 1 cup finely diced onions
- 1 cup finely diced celery
- ¼ tsp sea salt
- freshly ground black pepper, to taste
- 3 cups chicken stock
- 3 eggs, beaten
- 2 cups halved cooked chestnuts
- ⅓ cup raisins
- ⅓ cup finely diced dried apricots
- ¼ cup minced fresh tarragon
- 1 fresh thyme sprig, minced

GEAR

- 2 baking sheets
- large frying pan
- large bowl
- 1 or 2 large baking dish(es)
- foil

gravy + cranberry sauce

Rich turkey gravy, and a spicy cranberry sauce that'll punch you in the spleen, but in a good way.

servings: 3 cups gravy + 3 cups cranberry sauce | easy

GRAVY

Place a fine-mesh sieve over a small metal bowl and set aside. Transfer the cooked turkey to a platter. Keep only ¼ cup of fat in the roasting pan. Place the roasting pan over two burners on medium-high heat. Sprinkle the entire pan with the flour, and whisk vigorously to blend the flour and the fat together. Try to lift the brown caramelized bits stuck to the pan to incorporate them. Cook for 1 minute. Add the stock and continue to stir while the sauce reduces and thickens, 8 to 10 minutes. Carefully ladle the gravy through the fine-mesh sieve to strain. Season with sea salt and freshly ground pepper to taste.

SPICY CRANBERRY SAUCE

In a large pot, bring the water, cranberries, sugar, orange zest, and cayenne pepper to a boil. Stir, and cook just until the cranberries begin to pop and break open. Mix together, cool, and serve.

GROCERY LIST

- ¼ cup all-purpose flour
- 4 cups turkey or chicken stock
- sea salt & freshly ground black pepper, to taste
- ½ cup water
- 1 lb cranberries, fresh or frozen
- ½ cup raw sugar
- 2 tbsp grated orange zest
- ½ tsp cayenne pepper

GEAR

- fine-mesh sieve
- small metal bowl
- roasting pan
- large pot

turkey matzoh ball soup

Show me a person who doesn't like matzoh ball soup, and I'll show you a person who won't like this recipe. As for the rest of us, buon appetito!

servings: 6 to 8 | easy

TURKEY BROTH

Heat the extra-virgin olive oil in a large soup pot over medium-high heat. Add the carrots, parsnip, celery, and onion, and sauté for 8 minutes. Add the turkey bones and parsley, and cover with water — just enough water to cover the bones. Turn the heat down to medium-low, and simmer partially covered for 2 to 3 hours. Then strain the broth into a medium-sized soup pot using a strainer lined with cheesecloth. Discard everything in the cheesecloth. Simmer the strained turkey broth over medium-low heat, uncovered, for 15 to 20 minutes to reduce. Season with sea salt and freshly ground pepper to taste.

MATZOH BALLS

In a medium-sized bowl, lightly whip the eggs with the canola oil, ½ teaspoon of sea salt, and the cold water. Then, with a fork, stir in the matzoh meal and ½ cup of minced fresh dill. Refrigerate the matzoh ball mixture for 15 minutes. Bring a large pot of salted water to a boil. Take the matzoh ball mixture out of the fridge and with slightly wet hands, form the mixture into 1½-inch balls; then drop them into the boiling water. Cook for 20 to 30 minutes. Strain the matzoh balls.

SHKIAFFING IT TOGETHER

In each bowl place 1 or 2 matzoh balls, ladle on the turkey broth, and garnish with the remaining minced fresh dill.

GROCERY LIST

- 3 tbsp extra-virgin olive oil
- 2 large carrots, roughly chopped
- 1 large parsnip, roughly chopped
- 2 ribs celery, roughly chopped
- 1 large onion, roughly chopped
- bones of 1 roasted turkey, roughly chopped
- ½ cup chopped fresh parsley
- sea salt & freshly ground black pepper, to taste
- 2 eggs
- 1 tbsp canola oil
- ½ tsp sea salt
- 2 tbsp cold water
- ½ cup matzoh meal
- 1 cup minced fresh dill

GEAR

- large soup pot
- medium soup pot
- strainer
- cheesecloth
- medium mixing bowl
- large pot

pulled turkey sandwiches w/ bbq sauce

This is a turkey-licious take on a hot chicken sandwich — a Quebec staple. Tender pulled turkey meat is sandwiched between two slices of bread, then smothered with gravy and sweet peas… Come to think of it, Quebecers seem to douse everything in gravy: fries, sandwiches… The only thing that's got no gravy is the train. I had to punch that ticket in the good ol' US of A ;).

servings: 4 | easy

GRAVY

Melt the butter in a small pot over medium-high heat. Add the all-purpose flour, and whisk until the roux is amber colored, about 6 minutes. Remove it from the heat and set aside. Heat the extra-virgin olive oil in a medium-sized frying pan over medium-high heat. Sauté the onion for about 8 minutes, until the edges are crisp and golden. Deglaze the frying pan with the turkey or chicken stock. Whisk in the roux. Add the brown sugar, balsamic vinegar, cayenne, and sage. Turn the heat down to medium-low, and simmer for 15 minutes to thicken. The gravy is done when it coats a spoon. Season with sea salt and freshly ground pepper to taste.

PEAS

If using fresh peas: blanch them in a medium-sized pot of boiling salted water for 2 minutes, then drain. If using frozen peas: boil them in salted water for 30 seconds, then drain.

SHKIAFFING IT TOGETHER

Shred the mix of white and dark turkey meat with a fork. In a medium-sized bowl, combine the turkey meat with half of the hot gravy. Toast the bread slices. Divide the turkey equally among 4 slices of bread. Close the sandwiches with the remaining slices and smother each sandwich with gravy. Cover the sandwiches with peas. Serve immediately.

GROCERY LIST

- *¼ cup unsalted butter*
- *¼ cup all-purpose flour*
- *1 tbsp extra-virgin olive oil*
- *1 medium yellow onion, cut into small dice*
- *4 cups turkey broth (see page 69) or chicken stock*
- *2 tsp dark brown sugar*
- *2 tbsp aged balsamic vinegar*
- *½ tsp cayenne pepper*
- *¼ tsp dried sage, or 2 leaves fresh sage, minced*
- *sea salt and freshly ground black pepper, to taste*
- *1 cup sweet peas, fresh or frozen*
- *4 cups cooked turkey meat (white and dark)*
- *8 slices crusty bread*

GEAR

- *small pot*
- *medium frying pan*
- *medium pot*
- *medium mixing bowl*

nonna recipe showdown

My grandmas were funny-looking ladies. It's like when the *Nonna mold was created, someone forgot to carve it. As tall as they were wide, these tanklike women were built for another time: a time when you pressed olive oil with your bare hands, ground semolina with your teeth, and walked 679 miles to the water well every day with two babies permanently latched onto your boobs. They don't build 'em like that anymore (thank *bog, I already have enough trouble shopping for jeans as it is).

For my Nonnas, food wasn't a form of expression, it was their *only* form of expression. With four kids and a shmata sweatshop salary, back then immigrants didn't have time for frivolous things like "talking" or "affection." Their only priority was to put food on the table, so that became their language. If you were happy: lasagna. If you were angry: lasagna. If you had to talk, you sucked it up and talked about lasagna. So when food is your vocabulary you inevitably become fluent, and this chapter is dedicated to Nonna's prose.

In this section you'll find the best dishes I've ever eaten, not just from my grandmas, but from random grandmas I've kidnapped along the way. These grandma-tastic recipes are so epic, you can actually taste the guilt from not calling them often. Mmm.

nadmit

One thing I love about grandmas is they always have some kinda candy in their purse (along with crumpled tissues that make you wonder "are these used?") Nonna Carmela used to give me anise candies, and Nonna Theresa used to give me the creeps.

nonna's penne al forno

This penne pie was my Nonna Carmela's specialty. Well that, and saying "Ye, ye, ye" when she didn't understand a word you were saying.

servings: 6 | easy

BOLOGNESE

Heat the extra-virgin olive oil in a large saucepan over medium heat. Add the garlic and the chile flakes, and sauté for about 1 minute, until the garlic is golden and fragrant. Add the red onion and sauté for 8 to 10 minutes, until the onion has some crispy edges. Add the ground sirloin and sauté for 5 to 7 minutes, until the beef crumbles. Pour in the plum tomatoes, and then add the parsley, oregano, bay leaf, raw sugar, sea salt, and freshly ground pepper. Stir and simmer for 15 minutes, partially covered.

PASTA

Cook the penne in a large pot of boiling salted water until almost al dente, about 10 minutes. You don't want to fully cook the pasta because you'll also be baking it. Drain.

SHKIAFFING IT TOGETHER

Preheat the oven to 350°F. Add the penne to a large bowl, and mix in half of the bolognese sauce. Generously grease a baking dish with the unsalted butter. Add a 1-inch layer of penne, ½ cup of sauce, ⅓ cup of grated mozzarella, and a heaping tablespoon of grated Parmigiano. Repeat this until all the pasta is used. Top it off with grated mozzarella and Parmigiano cheese. Bake in the oven for 30 minutes, until the cheese is golden and bubbling.

GROCERY LIST

- 1 tbsp extra-virgin olive oil
- 2 garlic cloves, smashed
- ½ tsp chile flakes
- 1 red onion, minced
- 1 lb ground sirloin
- 3 cups canned San Marzano plum tomatoes, hand-crushed
- ¼ cup minced fresh parsley
- ½ tsp dry oregano
- 1 bay leaf
- ½ tbsp raw sugar
- ½ tbsp sea salt
- ¼ tsp freshly ground black pepper
- 1 lb penne (1 package)
- 1 tbsp unsalted butter
- 1 cup finely grated mozzarella
- ½ cup finely grated Parmigiano

GEAR

- large saucepan
- large pot
- large mixing bowl
- large baking dish (15" x 10", 2" to 3" deep)

nadmit

This penne al forno is so awesome, my family used to literally fight over the crisped corners...and my tattoos, and how I should get a real job instead of making "stupide videos" on the internet. Who's laughing now, eh? ...They are. I have some ridiculous tattoos.

tanja's cabbage rolls

Tanja is one of the coolest grannies I've ever met. Her home is filled with exquisite hand-crafted European toys, the kind of toys that make you wonder how much *your* Nonna loved you when she handed you a doily and a buncha expired rosette chocolates and yelled, "Play."

servings: 4 to 6 | intermediate

CABBAGE

Bring a large pot half-filled with water to a boil. Discard the outer leaves of the cabbage, and parboil 2 to 3 inner leaves at a time for about 5 minutes until you have 12 to 15 leaves. Delicately remove the leaves with tongs and place them on a dish towel to drain.

FILLING

Boil the white rice in a medium pot of salted water until al dente. In a large bowl mix the ground beef, cooked white rice, ketchup, egg, and sea salt and freshly ground pepper.

SHKIAFFING IT TOGETHER

Preheat the oven to 350°F. In a flat dish, lay down a parboiled cabbage leaf. Shape ½ cup of filling into an oval, and place it at the bottom of the leaf. Roll up from the bottom until the filling is covered, then tuck in the sides of the leaf and roll it all the way up, the same way you'd roll up a burrito. Place the roll in a casserole dish. Repeat with each leaf. Once the casserole dish is filled, pour the tomato-pepper sauce over the cabbage rolls, and bake them, covered, for 1½ hours.

GROCERY LIST

- 1 large savoy cabbage
- ½ cup white rice
- 1½ lb ground beef
- ¼ cup ketchup
- 1 egg
- sea salt and freshly ground black pepper, to taste
- 3 cups tomato-pepper sauce (see page 159)

GEAR

- large pot
- tongs
- medium pot
- large mixing bowl
- large casserole dish with cover

bibi's lentil + spinach soup

This comforting Middle Eastern bean soup comes from my girlfriend Hala's mom. Now Hala's mom isn't a grandma yet, but to the extent she's nagging her about it, I figured this chapter was a good fit for this recipe.

servings: 8 to 10 | easy

GREENS

Roughly chop the green onions, reserving the white parts for garnish. In a food processor, combine the onion greens, parsley, cilantro, spinach, half the mint leaves, and the dill. Pulse the greens until they're roughly chopped. You may need to open the food processor and carefully redistribute the greens so that the blade can reach them all.

SOUP

In a large soup pot, heat 2 tablespoons of extra-virgin olive oil over medium heat. Sauté the yellow onions for 10 minutes, until they're slightly golden. Add the garlic and turmeric, stir, and sauté for 1 more minute. Deglaze with the vegetable stock, and add the greens, chickpeas, red kidney beans, navy beans, and lentils. Stir and bring the soup to a boil; then reduce the heat to medium-low and simmer it for 45 minutes. Stir the soup every 10 minutes or so; this soup is very thick and needs to be redistributed to avoid scorching the bottom. At the 30-minute mark add a blend of ½ cup of sour cream and the all-purpose flour. Stir and season with sea salt and freshly cracked pepper to taste.

NOODLES

In a separate pot cook the spagettini in salted boiling water until al dente. Add ¼ cup of noodles to each soup bowl just before serving.

SHKIAFFING IT TOGETHER

Heat 1 tablespoon of extra-virgin olive oil in a small frying pan over medium heat. Sauté the reserved white parts of green onions and remaining mint until slightly crispy, about 5 minutes. Ladle the soup into bowls, put the remaining sour cream in a squeeze bottle, and crisscross the soup in a checkered pattern. Sprinkle with the crispy green onion and mint mixture, and with the sumac.

GROCERY LIST

- 2 bunches green onions
- 1 bunch flat-leaf parsley, large stems removed
- 1 bunch cilantro
- 1 cup baby spinach leaves
- 1 bunch fresh mint, stems removed
- ½ cup fresh dill, tightly packed
- 3 tbsp extra-virgin olive oil
- 2 medium yellow onions, diced
- 3 garlic cloves, roughly chopped
- 2 tsp ground turmeric
- 8 cups vegetable stock
- 2 cups canned chickpeas, drained & rinsed
- 2 cups canned red kidney beans, drained & rinsed
- 2 cups canned navy beans, drained & rinsed
- ½ cup dried green lentils
- 1 cup sour cream
- 3 tbsp all-purpose flour
- sea salt & freshly cracked black pepper, to taste
- ½ lb spaghettini pasta
- sumac spice, for garnish

GEAR

- food processor
- large soup pot
- large pot
- small frying pan

"Sumac is my favorite ways to spice things up! That and poppers. It is made from dried sumac berries, which have a tangy, citrus-like kick. So whenever you want to add subtle acidity to your dishes — but vinegar or lemon will overpower — think of sumac. It's fantastic sprinkled on soups, salads, eggs, rice, fish..."

great-grandma's salad niçoise

Everybody knows that salad is all about the dressing, and no one makes a better dressing than great-grandma extraordinaire — Dorothy Dorsey.

servings: 4 to 6 | easy

VINAIGRETTE

In a food processor, combine the Dijon, honey, garlic, cider vinegar, water, oil, sea salt, and ground pepper. Blend until smooth, thick, and emulsified. Set aside.

PEPPER-CRUSTED TUNA

In a frying pan, heat the canola oil over high heat until it smokes. Coat the tuna steaks generously on all sides with freshly cracked black pepper. Place the tuna steaks in the frying pan, and fry for 1 minute — don't move the steaks. Flip them over, and cook for another minute. Remove them from the pan, and set them aside to cool. Once they have cooled, slice the tuna against the grain into ½-inch-thick slices.

POTATOES, BEANS & EGGS

Cook the new potatoes in a large pot of boiling salted water until fork-tender, 12 to 15 minutes. Strain, and pop them in the fridge to cool. Once they have cooled, slice the potatoes in half, and toss in a small amount of vinaigrette. Boil the green beans in a large pot of boiling salted water until tender but firm, about 3 minutes. Strain, and place them in the fridge to cool. Once they have cooled, toss the green beans in a small amount of vinaigrette. Hard-boil the eggs, then cool them in the fridge and slice into quarters.

SHKIAFFING IT TOGETHER

Cover a serving platter with lettuce. Arrange the potatoes, beans, tomatoes, tuna, eggs, and olives over the lettuce. Sprinkle with the capers, and drizzle with the remaining vinaigrette.

GROCERY LIST
- 2 tsp Dijon mustard
- 2 tbsp honey
- 1 garlic clove
- ⅓ cup cider vinegar
- ½ tsp water
- ⅔ cup vegetable oil
- ½ tsp sea salt
- ¼ tbsp freshly ground black pepper
- ¼ cup canola oil
- 2 12 oz tuna steaks, sushi quality
- 3 tbsp freshly cracked black pepper
- 20 small new potatoes
- 30 green beans, trimmed
- 4 eggs
- 1 head Boston lettuce, torn
- 1 cup ripe cherry tomatoes, halved
- ½ cup olives
- ¼ cup capers

GEAR
- food processor
- large frying pan
- large pot
- large platter

a proposal for a proposal

So you fell in love, and it's time to pop the question. Now, you probably have *all kinds of romantic ideas on how to propose — like renting a Jumbotron, or waving a positive pregnancy test. But between you and me, nothing says "Marry Me" like a home-cooked meal. (Well, that and saying "Marry Me.")

Now, lots of people make fun of getting married. But let's face it, who's gonna massage your cankles when you're 60?! Folks, when you find a live one that loves you for YOU, seal the deal. It's not about rainbows, it's about insurance. I've always been pretty brass tacks about marriage. Maybe it has something to do with my parents sleeping in separate bedrooms ever since I can remember. (Don't worry, it was just the usual — Dad snored, and Mom hated him.) But despite these trivialities, they stuck with it! Because they knew that for better or for worse they had each other, and as the old Italian saying goes, "It's better to suffer together than to be happy alone."

Granted, some people are just plain terrified of marriage, and I gotta admit that whole "One-in-two-couples-get-divorced" thing is kinda scary. But look at it this way: "Two-out-of-two-couples-eventually-die!" Does that make you stop living? *Bein non. So on that depressing note, let's talk about ring costs…

Boys, pay attention: In the first year of your relationship you could propose with a twisty-tie and get away with it. But with every year that passes, your "boyish charm" starts competing with your "inability to clean the beard hair from the bathroom sink." Simple math: I'd say half a carat for every year you wait. So, let's get cooking.

nadvice

Proposing can be scary, but all good things are scary! …Well, some bad things are scary too, so what was my point again?

lobster bisque

This exquisite lobster bisque always reminds me to thank my lucky stars that I found my one true love years ago… ME.

servings: 6 | intermediate

LOBSTER STOCK

Remove all the meat from the lobsters, cover it, and refrigerate. Then chop the shells into quarters. Heat the extra-virgin olive oil and 1 tablespoon of unsalted butter in a large soup pot over medium-high heat. Add the red onions, carrots, celery, garlic, ½ teaspoon sea salt, and freshly ground pepper to taste and sauté for 8 minutes. Deglaze the pot with the white wine and brandy. Stir for 1 minute to reduce and burn off the alcohol. Now add the vegetable stock, tomato paste, parsley, thyme, bay leaves, peppercorns, and the chopped lobster shells. You want the liquid to just barely cover the shells; if there isn't enough liquid, add just enough water to cover the shells. Stir, turn the heat down to medium-low, and simmer partially covered for 1 hour.

DARK ROUX

Heat a small saucepan over medium heat. Add ½ cup of unsalted butter and the all-purpose flour. Whisk for 5 to 6 minutes, until it's amber colored and smells nutty. Take it off the heat and set aside.

BISQUE

Place a large colander into a clean, large soup pot. Line the colander with cheesecloth. Ladle in the lobster stock to strain. Discard everything in the cheesecloth. Heat the pot of strained lobster stock over medium-low heat. Add the roux, heavy cream, and saffron. Whisk to mix, and simmer for 15 to 20 minutes, until the bisque has reduced and thickened. The bisque should have a glossy sheen and coat a spoon. Season with sea salt and freshly ground pepper to taste.

SHKIAFFING IT TOGETHER

Sauté the lobster meat in 1 tablespoon of butter for a minute, just until heated through. To each large bowl add ¼ cup of warm lobster meat, and ladle in the creamy bisque. Garnish with chives.

GROCERY LIST

- 3 cooked lobsters
- 1 tbsp extra-virgin olive oil
- ½ cup + 2 tbsp unsalted butter
- 2 red onions, roughly chopped
- 4 carrots, roughly chopped
- 2 celery ribs, roughly chopped
- 6 garlic cloves, crushed
- sea salt & freshly ground black pepper, to taste
- 1 cup white wine
- ¼ cup brandy
- 2 quarts vegetable stock
- ⅓ cup tomato paste
- ¼ cup chopped flat-leaf parsley
- 1 fresh thyme sprig
- 2 bay leaves
- ½ tsp peppercorns
- ½ cup all-purpose flour
- 1 cup heavy cream
- ½ tsp saffron threads
- 1 bunch chives, for garnish

GEAR

- 2 large soup pots
- small saucepan
- large colander
- cheesecloth

"Lobster is da most romantic, but octopus is better at dirty talk. Anyways bro, here's how you cook a perfect lobster every time. Bring a big pot of water to a rolling boil. Throw in the lobster headfirst, and cover. The second the water starts to boil again, count 10 minutes for a 1-pound lobster, and 3 minutes for every pound after dat. Trust me, the last ting you need when you're proposing is an overcooked, rubbery lobster. Especially when you're already nervous about who da hell your parents arranged you wit! I feel you, and remember, you can always bleach a mustache."

balsamic baby back ribs w/ truffled baked potatoes

In my book there's nothing more romantic than tender ribs smothered in a Bitchin' BBQ sauce bursting with tangy aged balsamic, sweet maple syrup, spicy habañero peppers… Watch out, you may end up proposing to the ribs instead.

servings: 2 | intermediate

TRUFFLED BAKED POTATOES

Preheat the oven to 350°F. Wrap the russet potatoes in foil, and bake for 1 hour. When they are cool enough to handle, cut them in half, delicately scoop the cooked potato flesh into a bowl, and set the skins aside. Add the heavy cream, butter, truffle oil, green onions, ¼ cup of minced parsley, sea salt, and ½ teaspoon of freshly cracked pepper, and mix. Stuff the mix back into the potato skins, wrap in foil, and refrigerate.

RUB

In a bowl mix the brown sugar, smoked paprika, cayenne pepper, garlic, ¼ cup minced parsley, oregano, kosher salt, and 1½ teaspoons freshly cracked pepper. Preheat the oven to 325°F. Place each rack of ribs onto a piece of foil large enough to completely cover the ribs. Brush each rack of ribs with 1 to 2 tablespoons of canola oil, and massage with 1 to 2 tablespoons of the spice rub. Wrap the foil tightly around the ribs, place them on the baking sheets, and roast for 1½ to 2 hours, until the ribs are tender. Add the truffled potatoes to the oven for the last 45 minutes.

BALSAMIC BBQ SAUCE

Heat a small saucepan over medium-low heat, and add the apple cider, whiskey, aged balsamic vinegar, maple syrup, ketchup, red onion, garlic, and habañero. (Use latex gloves to chop habañero.) Stir, and simmer uncovered for 1½ to 2 hours. Turn the heat to medium-high for the last 15 minutes to reduce and thicken, stirring it often.

RIBS

Unwrap the ribs and slather them with the balsamic BBQ sauce. Place the ribs directly on the baking sheet and broil for a few minutes, until the sauce is bubbling and caramelized.

SHKIAFFING IT TOGETHER

Place the rack of ribs (either full rack or cut) on each plate, and serve with the truffled baked potatoes.

GROCERY LIST

- 2 russet potatoes
- ¼ cup heavy cream
- 3 tbsp unsalted butter
- 4 tbsp truffle oil
- 3 green onions, finely sliced
- ½ cup minced flat-leaf parsley
- ½ tsp sea salt
- 2 tsp freshly cracked black pepper
- ¼ cup brown sugar
- 2 tbsp smoked paprika
- 1 tbsp cayenne pepper
- 3 garlic cloves, finely chopped
- 1 fresh oregano sprig, minced
- 2 tbsp kosher salt
- 2 racks baby back pork ribs
- ¼ cup canola oil
- 1 cup apple cider
- 1 oz whiskey
- ½ cup aged balsamic vinegar, minimum 7 years old
- ½ cup maple syrup
- ¾ cup ketchup
- 1 red onion, minced
- 1 garlic clove, minced
- 1 habañero chile, minced

GEAR

- foil
- 2 medium mixing bowls
- 2 baking sheets
- small saucepan

raspberry trifle

Brace yourself, it's the last course! Now some of you may be tempted to hide the ring in the food. I never understood this strategy. I don't know about your partner, but I get so excited about dessert that chewing is optional. That being said, I suggest you present the ring on one knee, in a nonedible container.

servings: 6 to 8 | easy

CUSTARD

In a medium-sized bowl, whisk together the egg yolks, whole milk, ½ cup of sugar, and vanilla bean seeds. Heat the custard mixture in the top pan of a double boiler over medium heat, whisking constantly for about 30 minutes, until it's thick enough to coat a wooden spoon. Don't let the custard boil. Once it has thickened, cover and refrigerate it for about 2½ hours, until completely cool.

RASPBERRY JAM SAUCE

In a small pot, bring the water to a boil. Take it off the heat and mix in the raspberry jam. Set it aside.

WHIPPED CREAM

Using a hand mixer, whip the cream with ½ cup of raw sugar until stiff peaks form. Set it aside.

SHKIAFFING IT TOGETHER

Dip one side of each slice of pound cake in the sherry. Place a single layer of sherry-dipped pound cake onto the bottom of the trifle dish. Pour in enough custard to just barely cover the cake slices. Delicately disperse 4 teaspoons of the raspberry jam sauce and 2 heaping tablespoons of the defrosted raspberries on top of the custard. Repeat this layering until the trifle dish is full. Once the dish is full, use a butter knife to poke vertical channels into the trifle. Top the trifle with the whipped cream, and decorate it with fresh raspberries. Refrigerate it for about an hour to set.

GROCERY LIST
- *9 egg yolks*
- *4 cups whole milk*
- *1 cup raw sugar*
- *½ vanilla bean, seeded*
- *¼ cup water*
- *1 cup raspberry jam*
- *1 cup heavy cream*
- *2 loaves pound cake, sliced ¼" thick*
- *1 cup dry sherry*
- *3 cups frozen raspberries, defrosted*
- *2 cups fresh raspberries*

GEAR
- *3 medium mixing bowls*
- *small pot*
- *double boiler*
- *electric hand mixer*
- *trifle dish or large clear serving bowl*

remixed champagne kirs

Why get sucked into the same ol' boring Kir? At this point you're already signed up for a lifetime of "same ol' boring," so you may as well spice up the drink. Did I actually write that? What I meant to say was "MAZELTOV! YOU *NEWRDZ!"

servings: 4 to 6 | intermediate

MARINATED RASPBERRIES

In a medium-sized bowl combine the vodka, sugar, Thai chile, and peppercorns, and mix. Add the fresh raspberries and vanilla bean pod, and stir carefully so all the raspberries are covered in vodka marinade. Cover and refrigerate for 3 hours or overnight.

SHKIAFFING IT TOGETHER

Add 3 marinated raspberries to the bottom of each champagne glass. Pour chilled champagne over the top.

GROCERY LIST

- ½ cup vodka
- ¼ cup raw sugar
- ½ red Thai chile, sliced
- 4 peppercorns
- ½ cup fresh raspberries
- ½ vanilla bean pod
- 1 bottle champagne, chilled

GEAR

- medium mixing bowl
- champagne flutes

bitchin' party guide

I love throwing parties — so much so that if I wasn't doing *Bitchin' Kitchen*, I'd probably be in a band full-time. But trust me, "party planner" rings in at a close fifth. I get so delightfully absorbed by all the *newrdy details of party planning: the décor, the playlist, the activities, the food… It's a blast to create the perfect shindig (especially if you're a Type A personality with a mild obsessive disorder). Anyhoo, here's how I throw a Bitchin' Party:

BITCHIN' BUFFET Instead of fussing over a sit-down dinner, create a Bitchin' Buffet inspired by your favorite dishes that still rock at room temperature. By letting your guests serve themselves, you can actually have fun, and spend time on the important things: like catching up with friends, or the chardonnay.

ACTIVITIES We've all been traumatized by some peppy hostess-from-hell and her relentless charades regime. You don't wanna be that host. Find some fun activities like "The Anonymous Laugh Box": Depending on the theme of your party, print a question on a buncha cue cards. From "If you could change one thing about your partner" to "The crappiest Xmas gift you've ever received," have your guests anonymously submit the answer into a makeshift "Laugh Box," and take turns reading them out loud when sufficiently tanked. Laugh Boxes are as fun as Truth or Dare (minus the STDs).

DIY MIXERS BAR Stock a table with bowls of bite-sized fresh fruit and herbs marinated in liquor and simple syrup. Serve these gourmet mixers with chilled bottles of vodka, rum, white wine, and carbonated water. Your guests will have a blast experimenting with new flavor combinations, and you'll have a blast not having to play bartender all night. Just remember, folks: everything in moderation, *especially moderation.*

PLAYLIST Music can make or break a party. I've been to parties filled with awesome guests, but their "Sushi Lounge 2001" soundtrack had me gorging myself on cheese puffs in a quiet rage. If you don't have any musical taste, get a friend to make a playlist for you. Or better yet, put on my *Riot Grrrill* album. This will have your guests raging in no time, *in a good way.*

*Use your phone to SCAN NOW for a sneak peak of Nadia G's latest hits! (Just download a QR Scanner, you *newrds.)

red-hot roasted chickpeas – served like nuts!

Every time I see the "served like nuts!" part of this recipe title, it cracks me up. That random exclamation point kills me. Why the over-eagerness about these chickpeas' nut-like presentation? Or perhaps it's some rare form of foodie Tourette's: an uncontrollable blurting out, a garbanzo-bean-induced mania…Or perhaps it's darker, threatening… Who knows. I'll leave it up to you — to decide!

servings: 4 | easy

CHICKPEAS

Preheat the oven to 400°F. Dry the chickpeas in a dish towel or with a paper towel.

Toast the cumin seeds in a frying pan over medium-high heat until fragrant, about 1 minute. Remove them from the pan and grind them with a mortar and pestle, spice grinder, or knife. In a medium-sized bowl toss the chickpeas with the cumin, lime juice, cayenne pepper, chile oil, and sea salt. Spread the chickpeas in a single layer over a large parchment-lined baking sheet. Cook the chickpeas in the center of the oven for 35 to 40 minutes. Watch them carefully for the last few minutes to avoid burning. Every once in a while shake the baking sheet lightly to move the chickpeas around and encourage even browning.

SHKIAFFING IT TOGETHER

Let the chickpeas cool and serve these spicy, crunchy, high-fiber legumes like nuts!

GROCERY LIST

- 4 cups canned chickpeas, drained & rinsed
- 1 tbsp cumin seeds
- 1 lime, juiced
- 1 tsp cayenne pepper
- 3 tbsp hot chile oil (olive oil infused with hot chiles)
- 1 tsp sea salt

GEAR

- frying pan
- mortar and pestle, spice grinder, or sharp knife
- medium mixing bowl
- large baking sheet
- parchment paper

french green bean salad

A Bitchin' spread always needs something fresh and green…with bacon in it.

servings: 6 | easy

MARINATED LEMONS
Dice 15 slices of Marinated Lemons (see page 101). Retrieve all the onion slices and add them and the diced lemons to a salad bowl. Keep the remaining marinated lemons in the refrigerator for use in other recipes.

TOASTED WALNUTS
Preheat the oven to 350°F. Toast the walnuts on a baking sheet for about 10 minutes. Let them cool.

HARICOTS VERTS
Blanch the haricots verts in a large pot of boiling salted water for 1 minute. Drain the beans and immediately plunge them in an ice bath. Once they have cooled, drain the beans and add them to the salad bowl.

BACON
Heat a large frying pan over medium heat, and fry the diced bacon pieces until crispy and golden, about 10 minutes. Drain on a paper towel.

SHKIAFFING IT TOGETHER
When ready to serve, add the bacon, walnuts, and tomatoes to the salad bowl. Drizzle the salad with some of the oil from the lemon marinade, and season to taste. Toss and serve.

GROCERY LIST
- 1 cup walnuts
- 1 lb haricots verts, trimmed
- 8 slices bacon, diced
- 1 cup cherry tomatoes, halved

GEAR
- large salad bowl
- baking sheet
- large pot
- frying pan

marinated lemons

These marinated lemons taste as good as they look. Next time you're invited to a party, bring a jar of these suckers along as a gift.

servings: 6 to 8 | easy

SHKIAFFING IT TOGETHER

In a medium-sized bowl, toss the lemon and onion slices with the salt and sugar. Put the oregano sprigs and chile in a glass jar. Add the lemons and onions to the jar and pack tightly.

Fill the jar with olive oil. Close the jar and give it a good shake to distribute the olive oil, and then add more oil if there is still room. Close the jar again and leave the contents to marinate in the refrigerator for 2 days.

GROCERY LIST

- 3 lemons, thinly sliced
- 1/4 red onion, thinly sliced
- 2 tsp sea salt
- 1 tsp sugar
- 3 fresh oregano sprigs
- 1 finger hot chile, halved lengthwise
- extra-virgin olive oil

GEAR

- 1 medium mixing bowl
- 2-cup glass jar with lid

rockin' roast beef

Mmm, roast beef. What I love about roast beef is it's a one-pot crowd-pleaser that you can just *shkiaff in the oven and forget about. (Until it's ready, then I suggest you remember it.)

servings: 8 to 12 | easy

ROAST BEEF

In a roasting pan, place the beef fat side up and rub it with the ground mustard, 2 teaspoons sea salt, and 2 teaspoons black pepper. Let it stand at room temperature for 2 hours. Preheat the oven to 475°F, and brown the roast for about 15 minutes; then lower the oven temperature to 325°F. When the roast just begins to drip its juices, after about 1 hour, add the potatoes, onions, and mushrooms to the roasting pan. Check the temperature of the roast with a meat thermometer. Pull the roast from the oven when the interior temperature of the roast is 135°F to 140°F. Let the roast rest for about 15 minutes, then slice it thin.

CHIPOTLE MAYO

In a food processor, blend together the mayonnaise, chipotle peppers, ¼ teaspoon sea salt, and black pepper to taste.

TERIYAKI SAUCE

In a small saucepan over medium heat, combine the mirin, tamari, honey, sesame oil, crushed garlic, and ginger; stir and bring to a boil. Reduce the heat to low and simmer for 5 minutes. Strain the sauce to remove the garlic and ginger.

SHKIAFFING IT TOGETHER

Serve the sliced roast beef on a large platter surrounded with the roasted potatoes, onions, and mushrooms. Arrange the sauces, honey mustard, and prepared horseradish on the side.

GROCERY LIST

- 3-to 3½-lb boneless beef rump roast, first cut
- 1 tbsp ground mustard
- 2¼ tsp sea salt
- freshly ground black pepper
- 10 small potatoes
- 1½ cups pearl onions
- 20 mushrooms, whole
- 1 cup prepared mayonnaise
- 6 chipotle peppers in adobo sauce
- 1 cup mirin wine
- ½ cup low-sodium tamari soy sauce
- ¼ cup honey
- 1 tbsp toasted sesame oil
- 2 garlic cloves, crushed
- 8 1" knobs fresh ginger
- Honeycup brand mustard
- prepared purple horseradish (store-bought)

GEAR

- roasting pan
- meat thermometer
- food processor
- small saucepan

"Chipotle is dried smoked jalapeño. Typically 10 pounds of jalapeño make for only 1 pound of chipotle. Although it is possible to smoke your own chipotles using a home smoker, this is only recommended if you are an 'accomplished home smoker.' ... But in my home town of Raanana there is no such thing as an 'accomplished home smoker.' You're either one or the other."

cheese plate w/ candied walnuts

Everybody loves a cheese plate, but putting one together can be tricky. On one hand you wanna get creative with your selection; on the other hand you don't want your apartment to smell like someone died in it. Here are some of my all-time favorite cheeses. From the top going clockwise we've got: St. André, a triple-cream cheese from France. This baby is like Brie, but with an actual personality. Next up: a tangy Gorgonzola, an excellent mild(er) blue cheese. And last: a beautiful 4-year-old Gouda. This aged cheese is similar to a Parmigiano, dry and very nutty. Serve with honey, fresh fruit, and candied walnuts.

DIY vodka bar

This sexy DIY vodka bar always makes my parties a hit. Guests have a blast mixing their own custom cocktails and getting rowdy. As the old Italian saying goes, "If you're gonna be an ass, do it with class."

SIMPLE SYRUP

Bring the water and raw sugar to a boil in a medium-sized pot over medium-high heat, and simmer for 3 minutes to reduce slightly. Take it off the heat, and refrigerate until completely cold. Divide the syrup equally among 3 medium bowls.

MELON MIXER

Use a melon baller to make balls out of each melon. To a bowl of chilled simple syrup add the melon balls, mint leaves, and Midori liqueur. Stir and refrigerate for 30 minutes.

LEMON LIME MIXER

Zest and juice 6 lemons and 6 limes. To a bowl of simple syrup, add the citrus zest, vanilla, the juice of the zested lemons and limes, and the limoncello liqueur. Slice the remaining lemon and lime into ¼-inch-thick slices and add them to the bowl. Stir and refrigerate for 30 minutes.

SPICY BERRY MIXER

To a bowl of simple syrup add all the berries, sliced Thai chile, and Fragoli liqueur. Stir and refrigerate for 30 minutes.

SHKIAFFING IT TOGETHER

Serve the bowls of mixers alongside bottles of chilled vodka, rum, and carbonated water, and ice.

GROCERY LIST

- *3 cups water*
- *2 cups raw sugar*
- *1 watermelon*
- *1 cantaloupe*
- *1 honeydew melon*
- *½ cup fresh mint leaves*
- *½ cup Midori liqueur*
- *7 lemons*
- *7 limes*
- *1 vanilla bean, sliced open*
- *½ cup limoncello liqueur*
- *⅓ cup hulled and quartered organic ripe strawberries*
- *⅓ cup organic blackberries*
- *⅓ cup organic blueberries*
- *½ red Thai chile, seeded and thinly sliced*
- *½ cup Fragoli liqueur*
- *1 bottle vodka*
- *1 bottle rum (optional)*
- *1 bottle carbonated water*

GEAR

- *medium pot*
- *melon baller*
- *zester*
- *3 medium mixing bowls*

mille-feuille in a whiskey glass

Tender flaky pastry, delectable vanilla-infused custar, this dessert is… Ooh! Is that a DIY Vodka bar?!

servings: 8 | intermediate

PUFF PASTRY

Preheat the oven to 425°F. Lay the chilled puff pastry on a clean flat surface lightly sprinkled with all-purpose flour. Gently roll out the puff pastry until the dough is ⅛ inch thick. Place the dough on a baking sheet and let it relax in the refrigerator for 10 minutes. Using a whiskey glass as a mold, cut out 24 disks. Pierce the disks all over with a toothpick to prevent the puff pastry from rising too much during baking. Lay the puff pastry disks on a parchment-lined baking sheet and cook in the center of the oven until the disks are golden and crispy, 10 to 15 minutes. Let cool.

PASTRY CREAM

In a medium-sized bowl whisk together ⅓ cup of sugar, the egg yolks, flour, and ¾ cup of the milk; set aside. Heat a medium saucepan over medium heat, and add the remaining ¾ cup milk, remaining 3 tablespoons sugar, and vanilla seeds. Stir the milk until it begins to steam, 3 to 5 minutes. Don't let the milk boil. In a thin, steady stream whisk the hot milk into the bowl containing the egg yolk mixture. Pour the contents of the bowl back into the saucepan, and whisk over medium heat until it begins to thicken and large bubbles form, about 5 minutes. Remove it from the heat and transfer it into an ice bath to cool. Once it has cooled slightly, place the pastry cream in the refrigerator to cool completely.

ICING

In a small bowl whisk together the icing sugar and 1 teaspoon of cream. If the icing is too thick, add 1/4 teaspoon cream at a time until you get the right consistency.

SHKIAFFING IT TOGETHER

Line up 8 whiskey glasses. Place a puff pastry disk at the bottom of each glass. Spoon in 2 heaping tablespoons of pastry cream. Place another puff pastry disk on top of the pastry cream, then add another layer of pastry cream, and finish with a puff pastry disk. Drizzle with the icing. Chill and serve within a few hours, or serve immediately.

GROCERY LIST

- 1½ lb chilled puff pastry dough (preferably made with butter), thawed if frozen
- ⅓ cup + 3 tbsp raw sugar
- 5 egg yolks
- 4 tbsp all-purpose flour
- 1½ cups whole milk
- ½ vanilla bean, seeds separated from pod
- ½ cup icing sugar
- 1 to 2 tsp heavy cream
- ¼ cup blackberry or black currant jam (optional)
- fresh mint leaves (optional)

GEAR

- rolling pin
- baking sheet
- toothpick
- parchment paper
- medium mixing bowl
- whisk
- medium saucepan
- small bowl
- 8 whiskey glasses

depression desserts

Okay, so you're getting ready to bite into a rich, dark chocolate chip cookie. You're practically drooling over the warm fresh-baked goodness before you. You open your mouth wide and take a huge bite… only to discover that the chocolate chips are freakin' raisins! *Dizgraziate. You know exactly the kind of soul-shattering disappointment I'm referring to. What does this have to do with depression? Well, life is very much like a chocolate chip / raisin mixup. See, somewhere along the way we convinced ourselves that life's supposed to be all chocolate and roses. And it's this ridiculous expectation of everlasting happiness that sets everyone up for disappointment, which can ultimately lead to depression. But where did these unrealistic expectations come from?

Uh-oh. A little *her*story lesson. After the First World War, there were a ton of chemicals left over. Not wanting a precious drop of alkyl-dimethyl-benzyl-ammonium-chloride to go to waste, they created cleaning products to turn a profit. …And ultimately created "June Cleaver" to push those products — the happy housewife, enraptured with a life of crisp sheets and disinfection. The idea that women could achieve ecstasy by cleaning a toilet is ridiculous. But, as the age-old law of marketing goes, hear something often enough, and you'll buy it. Every woman bought it. And every woman was left holding the garbage bag, wondering why life stank.

Onwards. Feminism. Women entering the workforce. The sexual revolution. The pill. These product peddlers had to catch up, and they've been selling "Super Moms" ever since: a modestly dressed Suburban Susan climbing the corporate ladder with a duster and a smile. The problem is, we're still unhappy. Why? Well, I don't know. Maybe working two full-time jobs like running a household while maintaining a career and a sunny disposition ain't realistic?! So what's a girl to do? Only you have the answer to that question, and you need to think long and hard about what's going to give you real satisfaction. All I know is that you ain't gonna find the answer on the back of a fat-free cereal box.

In closing: life ain't a laundry detergent commercial where we **spend** our days running through lavender fields in slow motion, smiling like we just fondled Christian Bale on a private jet headed to Vegas. What? I like Vegas… *cough. Life is tough. And like the wise Denis Leary once said: "All you get is a f@cking cookie every once in a while." So let's bake some f@cking cookies.

inverted lemon meringue pie

When life hands you lemons, make lemon custard.

servings: 8 to 10 | intermediate

MERINGUE

In a large mixing bowl, combine the egg whites, 1 cup of sugar, white vinegar, and vanilla extract. Using an electric beater, whip the mixture until stiff peaks form.

Preheat the oven to 275°F. Using a paper towel, grease your baking sheet with the canola oil, making sure to get the bottom and the sides. Spoon the meringue onto the baking sheet, and delicately shape it into an even "crust" layer, bringing it up the sides of the baking sheet as well. Bake it in the oven for 2½ hours. Turn off the oven and leave it in there for another 30 minutes. The dissipating heat will finish cooking the meringue.

LEMON CUSTARD

In a large bowl, whip together the egg yolks, 1 cup of sugar, and lemon juice. Fold in the lemon zest. Heat a double boiler over medium heat, and cook the lemon mixture in the top pan, stirring constantly, until it's thick like custard. Remove it from the heat, cover, and refrigerate until cool. In another large bowl whip the heavy cream with ¼ cup of sugar until stiff. When the custard is cool, fold it into the whipped cream.

SHKIAFFING IT TOGETHER

Layer the custard mixture evenly over the cooled meringue. Cut, and serve.

GROCERY LIST

- *8 egg whites*
- *2¼ cups granulated sugar*
- *2 tsp plain white vinegar*
- *½ tsp pure vanilla extract*
- *1 tsp canola oil*
- *8 egg yolks*
- *⅔ cup fresh lemon juice*
- *1 tbsp grated lemon zest*
- *2 cups heavy cream*

GEAR

- *3 large mixing bowls*
- *hand-held electric beater*
- *rimmed baking sheet*
- *double boiler*

nadvice

Whenever I get overwhelmed, I just take a deep breath and try to find my happy place. . . . Then I remember I don't have a happy place.

chocolate cheese brownies

Brownies rule! And the tangy creamy goat cheese adds a, umm, tangy creamy goat cheese kick to a classic.

servings: 8 to 10 | easy

BROWNIE BATTER

Heat a double boiler over medium heat. Add 1 cup of unsalted butter and the dark chocolate to the top pan, and stir until the chocolate has melted. Once it has melted, take it off the heat and let it cool slightly. Whisk in 2 cups of brown sugar and 3 eggs. With a wooden spoon, fold in the toasted walnuts, all-purpose flour, and sea salt.

GOAT CHEESE MIXTURE

In a large mixing bowl combine the fresh creamy goat cheese, ½ cup of brown sugar, and 1 egg. Blend using an electric beater at low speed.

SHKIAFFING IT TOGETHER

Preheat your oven to 350°F. Grease a baking dish with 1 tablespoon of unsalted butter. Pour the brownie batter into the baking dish, then evenly disperse spoonfuls of the goat cheese mixture over the batter. With a knife, score the surface into a pattern. Bake the brownies for 40 minutes or until a test toothpick comes out clean. Cool them on a rack. Then cut into bars, remove from the baking dish, and refrigerate.

GROCERY LIST

- 1 cup + 1 tbsp unsalted butter
- 1 cup chopped unsweetened dark chocolate
- 2½ cups dark brown sugar
- 4 eggs
- 1 cup walnuts, toasted and chopped
- 1 cup all-purpose flour
- ¼ tsp sea salt
- 1 cup fresh creamy goat cheese, at room temperature

GEAR

- double boiler
- whisk
- large mixing bowl
- hand-held electric beater
- 9" x 13" baking dish

nadvice

When toasting nuts the trick is to stay focused because they can go from perfectly toasted to burnt in seconds. If you're not sure if your nuts are quite there, shake them around in the pan, or buy a yellow Mustang.

gooey goodness caramel cake

This old-school dessert ain't a looker, but what it lacks in the physical department it makes up for with rich, sloppy sweetness. Yup, it works that way with food too.

servings: 8 | easy

CARAMEL FILLING

Bring a large pot of water to a boil over medium heat. Drop in 2 unopened cans of condensed milk — yes, the actual cans — and simmer for 3½ hours. Remove the cans from the pot, and when they're cool enough to handle, open them and spoon the caramelized condensed milk into a large bowl. In another large bowl, whip the heavy cream with an electric beater until stiff. When the condensed milk is fully cooled, fold in 1½ cups of the whipped cream. Cover and refrigerate the remaining ½ cup of whipped cream.

SHKIAFFING IT TOGETHER

Grease a springform pan with the unsalted butter. At the bottom of the springform pan, place a single layer of Nilla wafers, filling the empty spaces with broken pieces of wafers. Place a 1-inch layer of the caramel filling over the wafers. Repeat with another single layer of wafers and another layer of filling until finished, about 3 layers. Refrigerate overnight. To serve, remove the cake from the springform pan, and garnish with ½ cup of whipped cream.

GROCERY LIST
- *2 cans sweetened condensed milk*
- *1 cup heavy cream*
- *1 tbsp unsalted butter*
- *1 lb Nilla brand vanilla wafers*

GEAR
- *large pot*
- *2 large mixing bowls*
- *electric beater*
- *springform pan*

rebecca's psycho pms chocolate balls

I got a taste of these babies at my friend Rebecca's place. One sweet and salty and nutty bite later, my taste buds and I both agreed that me and Rebecca would be friends for a long time.

servings: 22 chocolate balls | easy

CHOCOLATE MIXTURE

Heat a double boiler over medium heat. Add the semi-sweet chocolate, milk chocolate, and butterscotch chips to the top pan. Stir until everything is melted. Remove it from the heat, and fold in the peanuts and pretzels. Let the mixture cool slightly at room temperature.

SHKIAFFING IT TOGETHER

Line a baking sheet with parchment paper, and scoop on heaping tablespoons of the chocolate mixture. Refrigerate for 5 minutes. Remove it from the fridge, and with your fingers, gently compact the ingredients to form balls. Cover and refrigerate until you're ready to serve them.

GROCERY LIST

- 1 cup finely chopped semi-sweet chocolate
- 1 cup finely chopped milk chocolate
- 1 cup butterscotch chips
- 1½ cups unsalted dry-roasted peanuts
- 1½ cups crushed pretzels

GEAR

- double boiler
- baking sheet
- parchment paper

happiness = bacon

*I*n the last few years Bacon has exploded into super-stardom. Once just a humble breakfast side, Bacon has now risen to become the quintessential renaissance meat. Everywhere you look there's Bacon: clothing, air fresheners, perfumes, mints, cocktails, cookies… Even longtime A-lister Chocolate had to "get with it" and submit to Baconmania.

Bacon has gotten so famous, in fact, that when I wanted to make some pork candy on my show, I had to contact its agent at CAA. And although I'm a little jealous of its Q Score, Bacon deserves to be famous (but between you and me, it was trying a bit too hard at the James Beard Awards with that ridiculous cupcake outfit, pfft).

No food is as versatile as Bacon — constantly reinventing itself like Madonna or Lady Gaga, but with more sodium and less voguing. Bacon is "Pork for the People." Unlike bourgeois Foie Gras or Truffles, Bacon remains accessible despite its rise to fame. Its philanthropic scent and worldly taste bring smiles to faces young and old, rich or poor, beautiful or "after-six-vodkas-I'll-schtupp-ya."

We stand united under Bacon. Bacon, this chapter is for you.

candied bacon w/ cayenne

This candied bacon is so good, I'll leave you with a quote from our assistant graphic designer: "This photo of caramelized, crispy, sweet pig candy had me drooling all over the keyboard…and I'm a Jewish vegan" — Shirel Revah

servings: 6 to 8 | easy

SHKIAFFING IT TOGETHER

Preheat the oven to 400°F. Line a cookie sheet with parchment paper, and set it aside. Lay the bacon strips in a single layer on a wire rack, and coat the tops completely and evenly with the raw sugar. Lightly press the sugar into the bacon strips, sprinkle them with the cayenne, and transfer the rack to the lined baking sheet. Bake for about 12 minutes, or until the bacon is deep red and very caramelized. Check on the bacon frequently; the cooking time may vary depending on the thickness of the bacon. Use to`ngs to remove the candied bacon from the baking sheet, and transfer the slices to a wire rack to cool completely.

GROCERY LIST
- 16 strips applewood-smoked bacon
- ½ cup raw sugar
- ½ tsp cayenne pepper

GEAR
- cookie sheet
- parchment paper
- tongs
- wire rack

nadvice

Now the second these babies come out of the oven, you may be tempted to grab one with your bare hands, hide in a corner, and growl at whoever comes within a 3-foot radius of you. But watch out! Melted sugar doesn't burn, it maims, so take a deep breath, compose yourself, use a spatula to carefully lift them off, and let them cool and harden on a wire rack.

dirty carbonara

Creamy pasta loaded with crisp bacon bits and Parmigiano, what more could you ask for? I know, a jet pack. I too once yearned for a jet pack. But then I thought about the devastating crashes, the potential malfuntions 50 feet in the air…and all for what?! Just so I could "soar" to the corner store. Pfft. SO not worth it.

servings: 4 to 6 | easy

SAUCE

In a large bowl whisk the eggs and set aside. Heat a large frying pan over medium heat, and fry the bacon until it's really crispy, about 12 minutes. Using a slotted spoon, remove the bacon and place it on paper towels to drain. Leave 1 tablespoon of bacon fat in the pan, and add the unsalted butter. Sauté the onion until slightly golden, 2 to 3 minutes. Then lower the heat to medium-low and add the half-and-half and the cheeses to the pan. Stir and simmer until the sauce has thickened and all the cheese has melted, about 5 minutes. Don't let the sauce boil. Once the sauce is thick and smooth, remove it from the heat and let it cool slightly, about 2 minutes.

PASTA

Meanwhile, cook the pasta in a large pot of boiling salted water until it is al dente, timing it so that the pasta is done when the sauce is ready. Drain.

SHKIAFFING IT TOGETHER

While continuously whisking the eggs, slowly pour the cream sauce into the eggs. Add the hot pasta and toss quickly. The hot pasta will complete the cooking of the eggs. Add the bacon and the minced parsley, and toss. Season with sea salt and freshly ground pepper to taste, and serve hot.

GROCERY LIST
- 3 eggs
- 8 slices bacon, finely diced
- 1 tbsp unsalted butter
- 1 small yellow onion, finely diced
- 1½ cups half & half
- ⅓ cup finely grated Pecorino Romano cheese
- ⅓ cup finely grated Parmigiano
- 1 lb gemelli pasta (or fusilli)
- 1/4 cup minced flat-leaf parsley
- sea salt and freshly ground black pepper

GEAR
- large bowl
- whisk
- large frying pan
- slotted spoon
- large pot

split pea and bacon soup

I love this soup, but I gotta say split peas take forever to cook. In 1½ hours they barely achieve a toothsome al dente, which is the texture I've grown to love because it's all I have the freakin' patience for.

servings: 6 | easy

SPLIT PEA SOUP

Heat a large soup pot over medium heat. Fry the bacon until it's very crisp, about 12 minutes. Drain the crispy bacon bits on a paper towel, keeping the bacon fat in the pot. Add the unsalted butter and the onion, and sauté for about 8 minutes. Deglaze the pot with the chicken stock, and bring it to a boil. Then add the split peas, carrots, and celery. Stir, and simmer for 1 to 1½ hours, or until the split peas are tender and the soup is thick. Once it is cooked, stir in the maple syrup.

SHKIAFFING IT TOGETHER

Ladle the split pea soup into each bowl, and garnish with a big pinch of crispy bacon bits and some croutons (optional).

GROCERY LIST
- 4 slices bacon, finely diced
- 1 tbsp unsalted butter
- 1 onion, finely diced
- 8 cups chicken stock
- 2 cups dried yellow split peas, rinsed
- 2 carrots, finely diced
- 1 rib celery, finely diced
- 1 tbsp maple syrup
- croutons (optional)

GEAR
- large pot

soft little breads w/ bacon + onions

OMG. These soft little breads are so cute, you may wanna adopt them instead of eat them. (Trust me, they know how to snuggle.)

servings: 28 small rolls | intermediate

DOUGH

In a large bowl combine the warm water, yeast, and raw sugar and whisk to blend. Let it sit for 5 minutes. In another large bowl sift together 4 cups of the flour and the sea salt, and set aside.

Heat a medium-sized saucepan over medium heat. Add the milk, 3 egg yolks, and unsalted butter, and whisk until the butter has melted, about 5 minutes. Pour this mixture into the yeast mixture.

Make a well in the center of the flour and add the liquid. Using your hands, mix the flour with the liquid until a sticky ball forms. You made need up to ½ cup of additional all-purpose flour to form a ball that's not too sticky and can be kneaded.

On a lightly floured surface knead the dough for 10 minutes or until the dough has become elastic. Coat a large bowl with the canola oil, place the dough in the bowl, and cover with plastic wrap. Let the dough rise until doubled in size, about 1½ hours. Punch down the dough and divided the dough into about 28 golf balls. Cover with plastic wrap, and let them rise again until they've doubled in size, about 1 hour.

FILLING

In a small bowl mix the onion, bacon, and thyme. Take a dough ball, and gently stretch it out into a 3-inch-diameter flat disk. Place a teaspoon of filling in the center, fold the dough over the filling, and pinch it to seal. Turn it over seam side down, and gently form it into an oval. Place it on a baking sheet lined with parchment paper. Repeat with the remaining dough balls.

In a small bowl blend together a splash of water and 1 egg yolk with a fork. With a pastry brush lightly brush each roll with the egg wash.

Preheat the oven to 375°F. Bake in the center of the oven until the rolls are firm to the touch with a golden appearance, 10 to 15 minutes. Let cool slightly. Serve warm.

GROCERY LIST

- ½ cup warm water
- 1 tbsp active dry yeast
- 2 tbsp raw sugar
- 4 to 4½ cups all-purpose flour (or bread flour) + extra for kneading
- 1 tsp sea salt
- ¾ cup whole milk
- 4 egg yolks
- ½ cup unsalted butter, in small cubes
- 1 tbsp canola oil
- ½ Vidalia onion, finely chopped
- 6 slices bacon, finely chopped
- pinch finely chopped fresh thyme

GEAR

- 3 large mixing bowls
- whisk
- medium saucepan
- small bowl
- baking sheet
- parchment paper
- pastry brush

Try these little breads with beef! Fry 3 ounces of lean ground beef, half a finely diced onion, and 1 minced garlic clove until the beef is cooked. Once cooled, add ½ teaspoon minced fresh sage, season to taste, and use as the filling.

girls' night in

*I*n this chapter we're delving deep into the postmodern feminist plight. I call this chapter: "Mother Moonlight — Shave No More."

…OK. Now that most guys have turned the page — we're throwing a girls-only pajama party!!! Why girls only? Well most boys I know don't even own pajamas, so standing around with a buncha dudes in ripped boxer shorts is unbecoming. Plus, it's nice to chill with the ladies every once in a while. Think about it — if guys are always there, how can we talk bad about them?

Boy-bashing aside, I believe that spending quality time with your girlfriends is super-important, *especially* for all the ladies in relationships out there. A bit of downtime from your man is healthy. Let's face it, it's tough being hitched! You wake up, he's there. You're eating, he's there. You go to bed, he's there. …I guess that's kinda the point, but I don't get it. Then again, as the old Italian saying goes: "Men — you can't live with them…" …Nope. They're too messy.

Anyways, a PJ party is fun for *all kinds of reasons (mainly because you get to *shkoff like a savage in joggers). But why not take it to the next level with some kinda activity, like a clothing swap! *Bey yea! Just ask your girlfriends to bring Bitchin' stuff they don't wear anymore, and trade goodies after dessert! There's only one rule: No baby backpacks allowed. Just burn them and pretend the '90s never happened.

Let's get drinking.

We all know that "PJ Party" is just code for "gossip-fest," so here's the dirt: Did you know that when Panos found out that we were hiring Hans the Scantily Clad Food Correspondent, he wanted the gig? Yup, Panos was prepared for a career change, but he forgot to bring one thing to the interview — his 6-pack.

CAST YOUR VOTE
"Your loss, Nads. Why don't we let da public decide who shoulda been Da Scantily Clad Food Correspondent? To vote for me, email vote4panos@bitchinlifestyle.tv."

CAST YOUR VOTE

"Look, I like you, Panos, you're a decent dude. But seriously, you've got nuthin' on my magical sheen. Peeps, vote for the one and only Hans by emailing vote4hans@bitchinlifestyle.tv"

"Don't minding me . . . I think I am on the wrong page."

blood orange cardamom mojitos w/ basil

I'm not a fan of overly sweet drinks, desserts, or TV hostesses. In fact, I usually drink my vodka straight, because at the end of the day I'm just a simple girl who likes to get kicked outta bars in 3-inch heels. But since this is a PJ party and not a Motörhead concert, I figured, why not dress it up a little with a not-too-sweet blood orange mojito?

Servings: 12 cocktails | easy

INFUSED VODKA

Heat a small pan over medium-high heat. Add the whole cardamom pods, and toast them for 30 seconds, until slightly golden and fragrant. Set aside.

Pour the vodka into a medium-sized pitcher and add the toasted cardamom pods, blood orange zest, and vanilla bean. Stir, cover, and refrigerate for 3 hours or overnight. After the vodka has been infused, strain it and discard the cardamom, zest, and vanilla bean.

MAPLE BLOOD ORANGE JUICE

In a medium-sized pitcher whisk the blood orange juice with the maple syrup, and set aside.

SHKIAFFING IT TOGETHER

Pour 1½ ounces of infused vodka over some ice cubes in each highball glass. Add 4 Thai basil leaves. Pour in ⅓ cup of maple blood orange juice, and top with sparkling water.

GROCERY LIST

- 3 green cardamom pods
- 1 cup good vodka
- 1 tsp slivered blood orange zest
- 1 whole vanilla bean
- 4 cups blood orange juice, strained of pulp
- ¼ cup maple syrup
- 1 cup Thai sweet basil leaves
- 6 cups sparkling water

GEAR

- small pan
- 2 medium pitchers

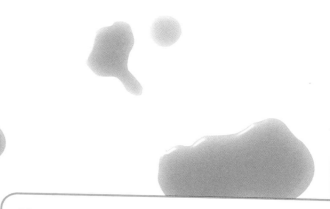

"I love pajama parties! Eating crumpets, drinking scotch, and making friendly conversations… What could be better? Oh I know! Not being alone when I do this. Do not worry about me drinking by myself, I learned many years ago that happiness is not found in the bottom of a bottle, but only halfway through the second."

gorgonzola risotto w/ portobella

This Gorgonzola risotto has got to be one of my all-time favorites. If I had to choose one dish to eat for the rest of my life it would be pulled pork with vinegar sauce. Man, that's good stuff.

servings: 4 to 6 | easy

RISOTTO

Pour the chicken stock into a medium-sized pot and heat to a simmer; keep it simmering over medium-low heat. In a large saucepan, heat the butter and olive oil over medium heat. Sauté the garlic for about a minute, until it's golden. Add the onion and mushrooms, and sauté them for 3 minutes. Stir in the Arborio rice, and cook for 2 more minutes. Then deglaze the pan with the wine and let it reduce completely. Once the wine is gone, add the simmering chicken stock ½ cup at a time. Let the rice absorb the stock, then pour in the next ½ cup, and so on, stirring constantly until all 5 cups of chicken stock are mixed in. This takes about 20 minutes.

SHKIAFFING IT TOGETHER

Fold in the Gorgonzola and Parmigiano, and stir for a few minutes until the cheese has melted. Add a generous pinch of sea salt, lots of coarsely cracked pepper, and mix. Serve in bowls, and garnish with a sprig of watercress.

GROCERY LIST
- 5 cups chicken stock
- 1 tbsp unsalted butter
- 1 tbsp extra-virgin olive oil
- 1 garlic clove, minced
- 1 yellow onion, minced
- 3 portobella mushrooms, diced
- 2 cups Arborio rice
- 1 cup white wine
- ½ cup finely diced good-quality Gorgonzola cheese
- ⅓ cup finely grated Parmigiano
- sea salt & freshly cracked black pepper, to taste
- ¼ cup watercress (optional)

GEAR
- medium saucepan
- large saucepan

nadvice

Mushrooms are like new boyfriends — you wanna make sure they're not rotting inside before you bring 'em home. Always sniff your mushrooms before you buy them; if they smell fishy, forget it. Seriously, don't be shy to remove the wrap and take a whiff. There's no need to be ashamed of publicly sniffing mushrooms when some stores are shameless about selling bad produce — especially pricey produce that doesn't move fast, like portobellas.

bacon chocolate

Bacon-Chocolate-Bacon-Chocolate-Bacon-Chocolate-Bacon-Chocolate-Bacon-Chocolate-Bacon-Chocolate-Bacon-Chocolate-Bacon-Chocolate-Bacon-Chocolate-Bacon-Chocolate-Bacon-Chocolate-Bacon-Chocolate. That's all the intro you need.

servings: 6 to 8 | easy

BACON

Fry the bacon in a medium-sized pan over medium heat until very crispy, 10 to 12 minutes. Drain the crisp bacon bits, and place on a paper towel to remove the excess grease. Pat with more paper towels; you want to remove as much grease as possible. Set aside and let them cool.

CHOCOLATE

Melt the milk chocolate in the top pan of a double boiler over medium heat. When the chocolate is 80 percent melted, take it off the heat, and keep stirring until all the chocolate is melted and smooth.

SHKIAFFING IT TOGETHER

To the melted chocolate add the bacon bits and Rice Krispies. Delicately fold it all in. Pour the mixture into silicone molds and refrigerate for 2 or more hours to set.

GROCERY LIST

- *6 slices maple-cured bacon, minced*
- *1 cup chopped good-quality milk chocolate*
- *½ cup Rice Krispies*

GEAR

- *medium frying pan*
- *double boiler*
- *silicone chocolate molds of your choice*

"Bro, you may be saying to yourself, 'Bacon chocolate?! What da f@#$?!' Eh — watch your language. Any gourmand (or PMSing wife) will tell you dat sweet and salty is where it's at. Just imagine: maple-cured bacon crisped to smoky perfection, den smothered in creamy milk chocolate... One bite and you'll say, 'Dis is f@#$ing amazing!' Eh — I told you, watch your language."

tiramisu cupcakes

Moist and fluffy cupcakes, topped with creamy espresso-mascarpone frosting… These cupcakes will definitely make up for the crappy romantic comedy one of your girlfriends is bound to bring over. (Just kidding — I have nothing against women who like romantic comedies, or men who dig action films for that matter. It's the fact that they reproduce that gets to me.)

servings: 12 cupcakes | easy

ESPRESSO GLAZE

Add 2 tablespoons of raw sugar to the hot espresso, and stir to dissolve. Add 1 tablespoon of rum and mix. Cover and refrigerate until cool.

CUPCAKE MIXTURE

Preheat the oven to 350°F, and position a rack in the center of the oven. In a large bowl beat the eggs with a hand mixer until they're foamy. Continue to beat the eggs while adding 1 cup of raw sugar in a slow and steady stream. Add 1 tablespoon of rum, and continously beat the egg mixture for 6 minutes, until pale and shiny.

In another large bowl, use a wire-mesh sieve to sift together the all-purpose flour and sea salt. Fold one third of the flour mixture into the egg mixture. Repeat two more times until all the flour is incorporated into the egg mixture. Delicately fold in the melted unsalted butter. Divide the batter equally among 12 lined muffin cups. Cook for 15 to 20 minutes, or until the cupcakes are slightly golden around the edges and an inserted toothpick comes out clean. Remove the cupcakes from the oven, and cool them on a rack. When the cupcakes have cooled slightly, brush each one generously with the espresso glaze.

ESPRESSO MASCARPONE ICING

In a medium-sized bowl combine the mascarpone, icing sugar, and the rest of the espresso glaze. Beat with a hand mixer until the icing is stiff. Using a pastry bag with a round nozzle (or a butter knife), ice each cupcake with about ¼ cup of the icing. Garnish each cupcake with 1 teaspoon of shaved dark chocolate. Place in the fridge for 1 hour to set.

GROCERY LIST

- 1 cup + 2 tbsp raw sugar
- ⅓ cup hot brewed espresso
- 2 tbsp rum
- 6 eggs, at room temperature
- 1 cup all-purpose flour
- ¼ tsp sea salt
- ⅓ cup unsalted butter, melted
- 2 cups mascarpone cheese (32 oz)
- ¾ cup icing sugar
- 2 oz 70% dark chocolate, shaved

GEAR

- espresso machine
- 2 large mixing bowls
- electric hand mixer
- wire-mesh sieve
- 12-cup muffin tin
- muffin liners
- medium bowl
- pastry bag (optional)

gluttony g-style

"The further I get, the farther I fall. I wanted this, now I want it all." — Nadia G, "We Won Big"

People always ask me, "Nads, what inspired you to get into cooking? And be honest — you have extensions, right?" Now, now…one question at a time please. What inspired me to cook is simple: hunger. As for the extensions: No siree *Pashquale. I was just born with naturally mermaid-like hair. It was a complicated delivery.

Anyways, back to the hunger, and on to the gluttony. I've always wanted more. For example, when I was a year old, I flew into a vein-popping rage because my uncle was *shkoffing a big plate of shpaghet', while all I had to slurp on was a bowl of broth — lack of teeth be damned.

As a teenager, I grew up in a conservative Italian neighborhood. It's not that I felt the grass was greener on the other side, it was kinda more like, "F@ck the grass, the picket fence, and the rewarding-career-with-benefits that goes with it." *I* was ravenous for rock-stardom. So while everybody else marched to the beat of "Ace of Base," I bought a guitar and shaved my head to "Rancid." When I reminisce about those days, all I can say is: "Man, I wish I remembered stuff so I could reminisce." Bah, after a stint in juvie, a coupla bad tatts, and even worse rock bottoms, I eventually learned a thing or two about the price of always wanting more. I learned: *I'll pay it.*

I spent my early twenties creating skit comedy. I guess comedy was a way for me to consolidate my suburban upbringing with my not-so-suburban perspective. It taught me that every dark cloud has a punch line, and how not to take things too seriously — especially myself. But there was something missing… the food. As much as I tried to get away from the "Italian Ting," the smell of Bolognese was calling me. But how the hell could I keep doing comedy, *shkoff some Bolognese, and still stay true to my rock n' roll lifestyle? Hehe. Enter *Bitchin' Kitchen*. Ladies and Ginos, I figured out how to make fun of my cake and eat it too.

But this chapter isn't about my stinkin' trials and tribulations. It's about gluttony, wanting it all, not looking down, and if you ignore the 30,000-foot drop for long enough, that tightrope becomes your highway… OK, the violins are getting too loud, let's get cooking.

buttermilk popcorn chicken

Is there anything better than fried chicken? Juicy, buttermilk-marinated chicken with a spicy, crispy crunch…mmm. What I love most about making this treat at home is that you actually get some chicken in your popcorn chicken.

servings: 4 to 6 | easy

CHICKEN

Cut the chicken breasts into equal bite-sized pieces. In a large bowl combine the chicken pieces, buttermilk, and 1 teaspoon of sea salt. Cover, and chill in the fridge for a minimum of 1 hour, and up to 8 hours.

BREADING

In a large self-sealing plastic bag combine the all-purpose flour, 1 teaspoon of sea salt, baking powder, cayenne pepper, oregano, turmeric, onion powder, and lots of freshly ground pepper. Seal the bag and shake well.

SHKIAFFING IT TOGETHER

In a heavy saucepan, heat 4 to 6 inches of oil over medium heat until a thermometer reads 350°F.

Remove one third of the chicken pieces from the buttermilk marinade with a slotted spoon, and shake them around over the marinade bowl to remove the excess liquid. Add the chicken pieces to the plastic bag filled with the breading. Seal the bag, and shake to coat all the pieces well. Remove each piece individually, and give each piece a quick shake to remove the excess flour. Carefully add the chicken pieces to the hot oil. Cook for 3 to 4 minutes, or until golden brown and cooked through. (If unsure if chicken is cooked, slice a piece in half to check that the center is no longer pink.) Once it is cooked, let the popcorn chicken drain on paper towels. Repeat with the remaining chicken. Serve popcorn chicken with maple syrup, BBQ sauce, or honey mustard for dipping.

GROCERY LIST

- 3 boneless, skinless chicken breasts
- 1 cup buttermilk
- 2 tsp sea salt
- 1 cup all-purpose flour
- 1½ tsp baking powder
- 2 tsp cayenne pepper
- ½ tsp dried oregano
- ½ tsp ground turmeric
- 1 tsp onion powder
- freshly ground black pepper, to taste
- canola or vegetable oil, for deep-frying
- maple syrup, for dipping (optional)
- balsamic bbq sauce (see page 89), for dipping (optional)
- honey mustard, for dipping (optional)

GEAR

- large bowl
- large self-sealing plastic bag
- large, heavy saucepan
- deep-frying thermometer
- slotted spoon

crazy rich linguine alfredo

This is one of the first dishes I ever learned to make. Alfredo sauce is ridiculously simple. Think about it — with that much cream, butter, and cheese, how can you go wrong?

servings: 4 to 6 | easy

PASTA
Cook the pasta in a large pot of boiling salted water until al dente. Drain.

ALFREDO SAUCE
Heat the unsalted butter in a large saucepan over medium-high heat. Sauté the garlic in the butter for 1 minute, until golden and fragrant. Deglaze the saucepan with the chardonnay, and cook off the liquid for a few minutes until it's almost dry. Add the half-and-half, and reduce the heat to medium-low. Stir often, making sure the half-and-half doesn't boil. If it looks like it's about to start boiling, take the pan off the heat for a few seconds and lower the temperature. Cook the half-and-half for about 5 minutes, until slightly thickened. Add the Parmigiano, and stir until the cheese has completely melted. Cook for another 3 to 5 minutes, until the sauce is thick, creamy, and smooth. Again, be careful not to boil the sauce. Once the sauce is done, remove it from the heat, and add the minced parsley, sea salt, and freshly ground pepper. Mix and cover.

SHKIAFFING IT TOGETHER
Toss the linguine with the alfredo sauce. Garnish with more minced parsley. Serve immediately.

GROCERY LIST
- 1 lb linguine (1 package)
- 2 tbsp unsalted butter
- 1 garlic clove, minced
- ¼ cup good chardonnay wine
- 1½ cups half & half
- ¾ cup finely grated Parmigiano
- ¼ cup minced flat-leaf parsley + extra for garnish
- sea salt & freshly ground black pepper, to taste

GEAR
- large pot
- large saucepan

"Most garlic is shipped all the way from China, and by the time it reaches your local supermarket it has begun to germinate, TO SPAWN! And this spawn is the root of all evils: indigestion, burping stinky, and Andy Dick's rise to fame…YA MANIAC!

But you can prevent this! Whenever you use garlic, cut him in half, and if you see garlic spawn, abort it right away! …In Raanana some people protest this operation: 'All garlic deserves a chance at life! What if he would grow up to be garlic president, garlic is a precious gift from G-d!'

And this is why I moved to America! Three times 'Pro-Garlic-Life' tried to kill me in Raanana! Why? Because I was the only one who dared perform this operation! I risk my life because I believe we have the right to choose an indigestion-free living! I believe that no one should be forced to burp garlic for hours in the night! I believe that Megan Fox should give me a chance. Just. One. Chance.

gnocchi poutine

This is Italian-Quebecois fusion at its best. Crisped potato gnocchi, smothered in a rich beefy gravy, topped with melted fresh cheese curds, *Miiiii, *estie.

servings: 4 to 6 | easy

ROUX

Heat a small pot over medium heat, and melt 3 tablespoons of unsalted butter in it. Add the flour, and whisk it together for about 6 minutes, until the roux is amber colored and it begins to smell nutty. Take it off the heat and set aside.

GNOCCHI

Cook the gnocchi in a large pot of boiling salted water for about 1 minute, or until they begin to float to the top. Once they float, boil for another minute. The water must remain at a rolling boil to fully cook the gnocchi. Do not let the water temperature drop by adding too many gnocchi at once.

Heat 1 tablespoon of extra-virgin olive oil and 1 tablespoon of unsalted butter in a nonstick pan over medium-high heat. Add the gnocchi in a single layer, and pan-sear them for about 1 minute per side, or until slightly golden. Repeat until all are seared. Keep warm.

GRAVY

In a medium-sized saucepan, heat 2 tablespoons of extra-virgin olive oil over medium heat. Add the minced shallots, and sauté until the edges are crisp and golden, 5 to 6 minutes. Deglaze the saucepan with the red wine, and reduce for 30 seconds. Add the beef stock, dried thyme, brown sugar, sea salt, freshly ground black pepper, and roux, and whisk together. Bring the gravy to a simmer, and let it reduce for 15 minutes, stirring frequently. In the last 45 seconds of cooking, mix in the cheese curds so they melt slightly. You don't want them to melt completely, just until they're soft but still whole.

SHKIAFFING IT TOGETHER

Plate a portion of pan-seared gnocchi (about 15 gnocchi) in each shallow bowl. Ladle on about ½ cup of the gravy and cheese curds. Lightly mix together and serve piping hot.

GROCERY LIST
- 4 tbsp unsalted butter
- 3 tbsp all-purpose flour
- 1 lb fresh gnocchi from an Italian specialty store
- 3 tbsp extra-virgin olive oil
- 2 shallots, minced
- ¼ cup good red wine
- 2 cups beef stock
- ¼ tsp dried thyme
- ½ tsp dark brown sugar
- sea salt & freshly ground black pepper, to taste
- 1 cup fresh cheese curds

GEAR
- small pot
- whisk
- large pot
- non stick pan
- medium saucepan

nadvice

A poutine isn't a poutine unless you use fresh cheddar cheese curds — which for the record should be beige, *not neon orange*. How did cheddar become neon? Well, cows are supposed to eat grass, and grass has an orange photosynthetic pigment in it called beta-carotene, which ends up in their milk. Milk gets concentrated when you make cheese, and *Tsaketa — the cheese has a golden tint. BUT with corporate farming, cows ain't eating much grass, so the cheese lacks pigment. What do they do? Add a bunch of exaggerated orange coloring which tricks you into thinking it's the good stuff. . . .So, just like strippers and spray tans, orange cheese is only enjoyable if you're in the dark.

habañero cheesecake

This is one of the best desserts I ever created. What I love most about it is that it's a fantastic basic recipe for any kind of cheesecake. Replace the key lime juice with melted chocolate, espresso, or keep it simple with just vanilla bean seeds, then top it with fresh berries…

servings: 8 | easy

CRUST

Preheat the oven to 375°F. Put the chocolate wafers in a resealable bag and crush them into fine crumbs. Pour the crumbs into a medium-sized bowl and add the melted unsalted butter; mix. Mold the crust onto the bottom of a springform pan, about ¼ inch thick. Bring it up the sides a little bit, about ½ inch. Bake for 8 to 10 minutes. Let it cool on the counter in the springform pan.

KEY LIME SYRUP

Bring the water and ¾ cup of raw sugar to a boil in a small pot over medium heat. Add 1/4 cup of key lime juice and the candied hibiscus flowers; stir. Reduce the heat to medium-low and simmer for 10 minutes, until slightly reduced.

CHEESE FILLING

Preheat the oven to 350°F. In a large bowl combine the egg yolks, 1 cup of raw sugar, ¼ cup of key lime juice, key lime zest, and habañero, and whisk together. Add the cream cheese and mascarpone; then mix with an electric beater for another 15 seconds. Set aside. In another large mixing bowl, using clean blades, whip the egg whites with the granulated sugar and the white vinegar until stiff peaks form. Delicately fold the meringue into the cheese mixture for 15 to 20 seconds. Don't overmix. Pour evenly into the springform pan, over the chocolate crust.

SHKIAFFING IT TOGETHER

Place 2 layers of aluminum foil in a large roasting pan. Place the cheesecake in the middle of the foil. Bring the foil up the sides of cheesecake to create a barrier wall around the cake; do not cover the top of the cheesecake. Pour water into the roasting pan, halfway up the sides of the cake (hence the impermeable foil barrier). Bake for 1 to 1½ hours. Allow the cake to cool completely on your countertop; then refrigerate overnight. Serve each slice of this cheesecake drizzled with a tablespoon or two of key lime syrup.

GROCERY LIST

- 1½ cups chocolate wafers
- ¼ cup unsalted butter, melted
- 1 cup water
- 1¾ cups raw sugar
- ½ cup key lime juice
- ⅓ cup candied hibiscus flowers (or dried cranberries as alternative)
- 5 egg yolks
- 1 tbsp grated key lime zest
- ½ red habañero pepper, minced, no seeds
- 2 cups whipped cream cheese, softened
- 1 cup mascarpone cheese
- 5 egg whites
- 3 tbsp granulated sugar
- 1 tsp white vinegar

GEAR

- resealable plastic bag
- medium mixing bowl
- springform pan
- small pot
- 2 large mixing bowls
- hand-held electric beater
- foil
- large roasting pan

makeover meals

The mere thought of certain foods can strike fear in our hearts: canned tuna, drab chicken, and, wait for it…MEATLOAF!!! Remain calm, because we're gonna give these dreaded dishes a Bitchin' makeover! And while we're at it, maybe even inspire *you* to throw out those nasty track pants. (Seriously, just throw them out.)

Ladies and Ginos, it's time for an upgrade! See, I look at food the same way I look at fashion: Invest in classic pieces, from sirloin to suits…then go wild with the spice, whether its za'atar or a zebra-striped scarf. And that's what this chapter is all about — taking a chance both in and out of the kitchen. (Well that, and showing off my awesome sequined shift dress. Cam'an, look at this thing! FYI: the back has a hot pink leopard pattern made *completely* out of sequins. It. Is. Sick.)

But some folks think that taking care of themselves is "vain and self-centered," that they "don't have time" for all this "narcissistic fashion crap." But you know what I think? I think *THEY'RE* the selfish ones! Do *they* ever stop and consider the visual assault of mom jeans on the innocent? Do *they* even care about the disturbing psychological effects of the "business-sock-and-sandal" combo?! You know, I have rights too! *I HAVE RIGHTS TOO, DAMMIT!!!*

*Mannaggia la miseria, let's get cooking.

nadvice

Express yourself because you only live once. Even if you believe in reincarnation, Louboutins don't come in dung-beetle sizes. As for heaven, let's just say fashion's lost on the toga crowd.

crispy tuna sliders w/ citrus slaw

Canned tuna can be depressing… although it has become slightly less depressing ever since they discovered that water purification plants can't filter out antidepressants, but I digress. Watch tuna go from blah to Bitchin' with these crispy tuna sliders: golden pan-fried tuna patties, topped with citrusy slaw, served on fresh mini buns.

servings: 8 sliders | easy

SLAW

In a large bowl combine the shredded cabbage, 1 tablespoon of raw sugar, and ½ teaspoon of sea salt. Toss it, cover, and refrigerate for 30 minutes to brine. In a jar, combine the poppy seeds, mayonnaise, 1 tablespoon of Dijon, lime juice, ½ tablespoon of raw sugar, ¼ teaspoon of sea salt, and lots of freshly ground black pepper. Close the jar and shake it until it's well mixed. Pour the dressing into the slaw along with ¼ cup of parsley, and toss.

TUNA PATTIES

Heat the olive oil in a large pan over medium heat. Add the garlic, chile pepper, rib of celery, cayenne, celery seeds, ¼ teaspoon of sea salt, and freshly ground pepper to taste. Sauté for 3 minutes, then take it off the heat and let the mixture cool for about 10 minutes. In a large bowl whisk together the egg, cream, 1 tablespoon of Dijon, green onions, ¼ cup of fresh parsley, the garlic-chile-celery mixture, and sea salt and freshly ground pepper to taste. Fold in the tuna and breadcrumbs. With lightly floured hands, shape about ¼ cup of tuna mixture into a patty. Repeat with the remaining tuna mixture. Dredge the patties in flour, and pop them in the freezer to firm up for 10 minutes. Heat ½ inch of canola oil to 350°F on a thermometer in a large frying pan, and fry the tuna patties for 3 to 5 minutes, until golden and heated through. Drain them on paper towels.

SHKIAFFING IT TOGETHER

Place each tuna patty onto a slider bun, and top with the citrusy slaw.

GROCERY LIST

- 1 small red cabbage, shredded
- 1½ tbsp raw sugar
- sea salt
- 1 tbsp poppy seeds
- ¼ cup mayonnaise
- 2 tbsp Dijon mustard
- 1 fresh lime, juiced
- freshly ground black pepper, to taste
- ½ cup minced fresh parsley
- 1 tbsp extra-virgin olive oil
- 1 garlic clove, minced
- 1 fresh red chile pepper, minced
- 1 rib celery, minced
- ¼ tsp cayenne pepper
- ¼ tsp celery seeds
- 1 egg, beaten
- 1 tbsp heavy cream
- 3 green onions, finely sliced
- 2 cups canned tuna in water, drained
- ⅓ cup dry breadcrumbs
- 2 tbsp all-purpose flour
- canola oil
- 8 slider buns

GEAR

- 2 large mixing bowls
- jar with lid
- large frying pan
- deep-frying thermometer

meatloaf w/ awesomesauce

I never ate meatloaf growing up, and the way people hated on it, I sure didn't feel like I was missing anything. Until I tasted this meatloaf. Oh man — juicy seasoned beef smothered in a tangy sauce. As the title suggests, this is by far the most awesome f'n meatloaf you'll ever have. Ever.

servings: 6 | easy

MEATLOAF

In a large bowl, combine the ground chuck, egg, onion, potato, ½ cup of Hunt's tomato sauce, breadcrumbs, sea salt, and freshly cracked pepper. Grease the baking pan with the butter. Form the beef mixture into a bread-like loaf and place in the center of the pan.

AWESOMESAUCE

In a medium-sized bowl combine ½ cup of Hunt's tomato sauce, mustard, brown sugar, vinegar, and water. Whisk and set aside.

SHKIAFFING IT TOGETHER

Preheat the oven to 350°F. Bake the meatloaf for 15 minutes, until browned. Once it is browned, remove it from the oven, and pour ⅔ cup of sauce over the meatloaf. Bake for another 1¼ hours, basting the loaf with the remaining sauce every 10 minutes. Once the meatloaf is cooked, remove it from the pan, slice it up, and serve.

GROCERY LIST

- 2 lb lean ground chuck
- 1 egg
- 1 yellow onion, coarsely grated
- 1 russet potato, finely grated
- 1 cup Hunt's tomato sauce
- ½ cup dry breadcrumbs
- 1½ tsp sea salt
- freshly cracked black pepper, to taste
- 1 tbsp unsalted butter
- 2 tbsp prepared mustard
- 2 tbsp dark brown sugar
- 2 tbsp plain white vinegar
- 1 cup water

GEAR

- large mixing bowl
- 10" x 13" baking pan
- medium mixing bowl

stuffed peppers w/ ground turkey

Lean ground turkey has become a staple in lots of households, and consequently, so has the fear of eating lean ground turkey. But peppers are a magical thing: they infuse the ground turkey stuffing with a juicy aromatic goodness that makes you wanna give your partner a wedgie. Not just any ol' wedgie though, one of my patented snap-back wedgies. Let me explain: first you roll down the top of the underwear a few times, and *then* yank them up into a wedgie. The rolled-down underwear confuses your partner, making them immediately try to roll their underwear back up, further wedgifying themselves. Oh yes. This is a great dish.

servings: 4 | easy

TOMATO-PEPPER SAUCE

Roughly chop 1 red bell pepper, and cook in a small pot of boiling water for 15 minutes, until tender. Drain and puree. Sieve the pureed pepper with the pureed tomatoes into a bowl. Season with the sea salt, raw sugar, and freshly cracked pepper. Set aside.

PEPPERS

Slice the top off of 4 bell peppers; reserve the tops, and remember which top goes with which pepper. Remove the seeds and pith from the inside of the peppers.

TURKEY STUFFING

Heat the extra-virgin olive oil in a large pan over medium heat. Sauté the onions for 12 minutes, until slightly browned. Add the ground turkey and cook for 12 to 15 minutes, or until cooked through. Stir in the grated carrots, zucchini, and ½ cup of tomato-pepper sauce, and take it off the heat.

SHKIAFFING IT TOGETHER

Preheat the oven to 350°F. Place the peppers in a deep baking dish, and spoon in the stuffing. Pour 1 tablespoon of tomato-pepper sauce over the exposed stuffing and crown each pepper with its matching top. Pour the rest of the tomato-pepper sauce into the bottom of the baking dish, and bake for 1 hour covered, and another 30 minutes uncovered.

GROCERY LIST

- 5 red or orange bell peppers
- 2 cups San Marzano plum tomatoes, pureed
- ½ tsp sea salt
- ½ tsp raw sugar
- freshly cracked black pepper, to taste
- 2 tbsp extra-virgin olive oil
- 2 small yellow onions, finely chopped
- 1½ lb ground turkey
- 2 carrots , grated
- 2 zucchini, grated

GEAR

- small pot
- sieve
- medium mixing bowl
- large frying pan
- deep baking dish

nadvice

This recipe is excellent with ground beef or veal. If you wanna go veg, replace the meat with par-cooked rice and beans.

juicy roasted chicken

I'm gonna be honest with you: chicken can be pretty freakin' boring. But this roasted chicken stuffed with lemon, onion, and herbs will guarantee a juicy bird with crispy skin every time.

servings: 4 to 6 | easy

ROASTED CHICKEN

Preheat the oven to 425°F. Discard the chicken gizzards (or use them for another recipe you won't find in this book :P). Rinse the chicken in cold water and pat dry. Place the chicken on a wire rack in a roasting pan. Stuff the chicken's cavity with the lemon, onion, garlic cloves, rosemary, thyme, oregano, and parsley.

Using a sharp knife, slice the chicken's skin in various places, inserting little pats of butter under the skin; this will make the skin extra-crispy. Now massage the whole bird with the extra-virgin olive oil, smoked paprika, sea salt, and freshly cracked pepper.

Roast the chicken in the oven for 45 minutes. Then place the chicken on a large platter, tent it with foil, and let it rest for 10 minutes before serving.

GROCERY LIST
- 1 whole chicken
- 1 lemon, halved
- 1 yellow onion, quartered
- 6 garlic cloves
- 1 fresh rosemary sprig
- 1 fresh thyme sprig
- 1 fresh oregano sprig
- 4 fresh parsley sprigs
- 2 tbsp unsalted butter
- 3 tbsp extra-virgin olive oil
- 1 tbsp smoked paprika
- ½ tbsp sea salt
- freshly cracked black pepper, to taste

GEAR
- roasting pan with wire rack insert
- foil

"There're basically three types of chicken out dere. Let's start with 'Free Range.' These chickens are da ones that are allowed to move around, but how much space dey have to spread those wings depends on da farmer's definition of 'free.' Some chickens get a coupla feet of dirt and gravel, others get a whole pasture to party in. But how do you know which chickens danced around da most? You don't, unless you deal directly with da farmer.

Now let's talk 'Grain Fed' chicken: dis is only a marketing term, because pretty much all chickens eat grain. But what kinda grain is a whole other story...

Which brings us to the polar opposite: 'Organic Chicken.' These babies are always raised without antibiotics, eat organic pesticide-free grain, and are da chickens of the Gods! Between you and me: you want your chickens to live a good life...Psst! There are over 20 billion chickens in da world. Dat's 4 angry chickens for every man...Sometimes at night, I can't sleep! What if da chickens ever wanted revenge?! If they planned it good and attacked us in da night, they could win, *bro. Tink about it."

spicy chicken barley risotto w/ dried currants and smoked gouda

What I love most about roasted chicken is that you can make a buncha meals out of it. Take a roasted chicken and turn it into a saucy, spicy barley risotto loaded with shredded breast meat, smoked Gouda, and sweet currants. Then use the bones to make a stock. Then use the stock to make a soup. Then use the soup to make a sauce reduction…you get the picture, and it tastes like roasted chicken. A-hem. On to the recipe.

servings: 4 to 6 | easy

BARLEY

Cook the pearl barley in an uncovered medium saucepan of boiling salted water until tender, 1 to 1½ hours, adding water as needed.

SPICY TOMATO SAUCE

In a large saucepan, heat the extra-virgin olive oil over medium heat. Add the garlic and jalapeño, and sauté for 2 minutes, until fragrant. Now add the shallots and smoked paprika, and sauté for 5 more minutes. Deglaze the saucepan with the red wine, stir, and reduce for 2 minutes. Then add the crushed tomatoes, 1 cup of chicken stock, bay leaf, thyme, oregano, raw sugar, sea salt, and freshly ground pepper. Stir and simmer, partially covered, for 20 minutes.

SHKIAFFING IT TOGETHER

To the sauce, add the cooked barley, smoked Gouda, shredded chicken breast, and currants. Turn the heat down to medium-low, and delicately mix for a few minutes until the cheese has melted.

GROCERY LIST

- 1 cup pearl barley
- 2 tbsp extra-virgin olive oil
- 2 garlic cloves, minced
- 1 jalapeño pepper, minced
- 3 shallots, minced
- ½ tbsp smoked paprika
- ¼ cup good red wine
- 2 cups canned San Marzano plum tomatoes, hand-crushed
- 1 cup chicken stock
- 1 bay leaf
- ¼ tsp dried thyme
- ¼ tsp dried oregano
- ½ tbsp raw sugar
- ¼ tsp sea salt
- freshly cracked black pepper, to taste
- ½ cup finely grated smoked Gouda
- 1 roasted chicken breast, shredded (see page 161)
- ½ cup dried currants or raisins

GEAR

- medium saucepan
- large saucepan

back-of-the-fridge bachelorfest

The great Tyler Durden once said: "You are not a beautiful or unique snowflake, you are the same organic decaying matter as everything else." You know why he said that? Because you are what you eat, and that bachelor fridge is nasty! Pre-minced garlic, ketchup, and Patrón. This ain't a rap song, son, it's a cry for help.

Look, I know that sometimes what lurks in the back of our fridge ain't too inspiring… unless it's been there long enough to strike up a conversation. That's why in this chapter we're gonna conquer the challenge of the bachelor fridge! The good news is that some of the tastiest dishes in the world are peasant dishes, so you don't need fancy-pants ingredients to make a good meal. All you really need is some elbow grease, some old-school know-how, and potatoes. (You have potatoes, right? Aw, man! How can you not have potatoes?!) Anyways, whether you're a broke-ass farmer or a lazy-ass bachelor, it can all amount to some epic grub if you're willing to put in the effort (and get some potatoes).

Look, I know that starting to cook for yourself can be scary, but it's exciting too! Some of my most adventurous experimentation went down when I first moved out. Ditto for the cooking. Crumbled chips in rose sauce? Been there, barfed that. Pesto made with wilted parsley and beer nuts? I *shkoffed it. The point is: go wild, have fun in the kitchen! Who knows, you may just end up with a new Bitchin' recipe! Or indigestion. Either way.

Let's get cooking.

nadvice

Stand tall, bachelor/ettes! Next time you stare blankly into the fridge, hopelessly wondering why that molding slice of pizza hasn't made babies yet, know that you have the power to whip something up from scratch! It may not be a rack of lamb, but things could be worse. You could be married.

sartù di patate

Nothing but some eggs, cheese, and a coupla potatoes? I'm gonna show you how to make my *zia's scrumptious Sartù di Patate potato cake. If you don't have smoked Scamorza cheese handy, feel free to use cheddar, Swiss — pretty much any cheese you have in the fridge will do, except for that stuff that turned into cheese a few weeks ago.

servings: 6 | easy

POTATOES

Cook the cubed russets in a large pot of boiling salted water until fork-tender, about 15 minutes. Drain and let cool. Pass the russets through a ricer into a big bowl. If you don't have a ricer, you can mash them up by hand. Set aside and let cool for 15 minutes.

SAUSAGE

In a frying pan, heat the extra-virgin olive oil over medium heat. Remove the sausage meat from the casings, crumble into small pieces, and fry it for 10 to 15 minutes, until the meat is crispy and caramelized. Drain the fat. Set aside and let cool for 10 minutes.

POTATO MIXTURE

In a large bowl, whisk together the eggs, mozzarella, and Grana Padano cheese (if you don't have any Grana Padano, you can use Parmigiano). Fold in the crisped sausage bits, riced russets, parsley, sea salt, and lots of freshly cracked pepper. Mix until all the ingredients are evenly incorporated.

SHKIAFFING IT TOGETHER

Grease the baking dish with 1 tablespoon of unsalted butter. Add half the potato mixture in an even layer. Then add an even layer of the smoked Scamorza. Now top it off with the remaining potato mixture. Add small pats of the remaining 2 tablespoons unsalted butter to the top. Sprinkle the top with the breadcrumbs, and bake at 350°F for 30 minutes, until the crust is golden.

GROCERY LIST

- 8 large russet potatoes, cubed
- 1 tsp extra-virgin olive oil
- 2 spicy Italian sausages
- 3 eggs, beaten
- ⅓ cup finely grated mozzarella
- ⅓ cup finely grated Grana Padano
- ¼ cup minced fresh parsley
- 1 tsp sea salt
- freshly cracked black pepper, to taste
- 3 tbsp unsalted butter
- ½ lb smoked Scamorza cheese, sliced into ¼"-thick rounds
- 3 tbsp Italian seasoned breadcrumbs

GEAR

- large pot
- potato ricer (optional)
- 2 large mixing bowls
- large frying pan
- 9" x 13" baking dish

"Just for the record, not all bachelors live like savages. *Me I always had *all kinds of good food in the fridge. OK, so maybe I lived with my mother until I got married… But that's not the point, the point is…Italian sausages! Now, real Italian sausages should be red, not pink, *bro. You're looking for 85% pork shoulder meat, 15% fat. But if you don't have sausages, you could use any charcuterie: soppressata, salame di Genoa, or bacon even…whatever you have in the fridge (or mom's fridge ;)."

pasta frittata

Crispy pasta + fluffy eggs + whatever leftovers you have = dinner.

servings: 6 | easy

FRITTATA

Preheat the oven to 350°F, and position a rack in the center of the oven. In a medium-sized bowl, whisk together the eggs and heavy cream. Add the sea salt, freshly ground pepper, cayenne, and Romano cheese, and whisk for a minute more. Heat the extra-virgin olive oil and unsalted butter in a large ovenproof frying pan over medium-high heat. Add the green onions and garlic, and sauté for 1 minute. Add the pasta and sauté for 3 minutes or until the pasta starts to crisp slightly. Once the pasta is slightly crispy and golden, add the spinach and Black Forest ham. Lightly mix.

SHKIAFFING IT TOGETHER

Pour the egg mixture into the pan, and give the pan a little shake to evenly distribute the egg mixture. Let it cook for 2 minutes on the stovetop. Transfer the pan to the oven, and cook until the center of the frittata is firm, about 25 minutes. Let the frittata cool slightly and cut it into wedges. This frittata is also delicious served cold or at room temperature.

GROCERY LIST

- *3 eggs*
- *¼ cup heavy cream (or whole milk)*
- *¼ tsp sea salt*
- *freshly ground black pepper, to taste*
- *¼ tsp cayenne pepper*
- *½ cup finely grated romano cheese*
- *1 tbsp extra-virgin olive oil*
- *1 tbsp unsalted butter*
- *3 green onions, sliced into thin rounds*
- *2 garlic cloves, minced*
- *3 cups leftover spaghetti (make pasta day before, and bring to room temperature before cooking)*
- *½ cup baby spinach, julienned*
- *4 slices good-quality Black Forest ham, julienned same size as baby spinach*

GEAR

- *medium mixing bowl*
- *whisk*
- *large ovenproof frying pan*

bachelor pad thai

If you like peanut butter dumplings, you'll love this quick and dirty pad thai. Yup, there other uses for peanut butter besides savagely spooning it into your mouth in a munchie meltdown.

servings: 4 | easy

PEANUT SAUCE

In a medium-sized bowl, combine the peanut butter, lime juice, and water. Whisk vigorously for 5 minutes, until it emulsifies into a creamy sauce. Add the maple syrup, aged balsamic vinegar, and red Thai chile, and whisk for 1 more minute. The sauce should be smooth and creamy. Set it aside.

PASTA

Cook the tubettini pasta in a large pot of salted water until al dente, then strain. In a large saucepan, heat the canola oil over medium heat. Sauté the garlic and ginger for 1 minute. Add the cooked tubettini, drizzle with the soy sauce, and mix. Shake the pan so the pasta doesn't stick. Cook like this for about 2 minutes, then turn the heat down to medium-low, add the peanut sauce, mix, and cook for 1 to 2 more minutes.

SHKIAFFING IT TOGETHER

Plate the pasta. Sprinkle with green onions, crushed peanuts (optional), and minced cilantro. Serve with lime wedges.

GROCERY LIST

- ¾ cup crunchy peanut butter
- 3 limes, juiced
- 3 tbsp water
- 3 tbsp maple syrup
- 1 tbsp aged balsamic vinegar (minimum 7 years old)
- 1 red Thai chile, sliced into thin rounds
- 1 lb tubettini pasta
- ¼ cup canola oil
- 2 garlic cloves, peeled and crushed
- 1 1" knob fresh ginger, crushed with a garlic press
- 1 tbsp soy sauce
- 2 green onions, sliced into thin rounds (use mostly the green part.)
- crushed peanuts (optional)
- ¼ cup cilantro leaves, minced
- lime wedges

GEAR

- medium mixing bowl
- whisk
- large pot
- large saucepan

Be patient when whisking the peanut butter mixture. At first it'll feel like it'll never come together, but after a minute or so it'll emulsify, promise.

sweet arancini w/ leftover steamed rice

Yea, yea, arancini are usually made with leftover risotto. But let's get real here — when you *shkoff risotto, you have leftovers? Exactly. Steamed rice it is.

servings: 6 | easy

CUSTARD

In a medium-sized bowl whisk together the egg yolks and raw sugar, and set it aside. Heat a small saucepan over medium heat Add the heavy cream and the vanilla seeds, and stir constantly for about 8 minutes, or until tiny bubbles form along the edges. Be careful not to let it boil. Slowly add the hot cream to the sugary yolks, one tablespoon at a time. Take your time, you don't want to cook the yolks.

Pour the egg mixture back into the saucepan, turn the heat down to medium-low, and stir constantly. If it looks like it's starting to boil, just lift the pot off the burner for a few seconds and keep stirring. Do this for 5 to 8 minutes, until the custard is thick enough to coat a wooden spoon. Transfer the pan to an ice bath, and stir some more to cool and further thicken.

SWEET ARANCINI

Pour the cooled custard into a large bowl and mix in the cold rice, chopped raisins, ¼ teaspoon of cinnamon, and nutmeg. Cover and refrigerate this mixture for 30 minutes. Once it has cooled, dip your hands in a bowl of water to prevent the rice from sticking, and roll the mixture into little golf balls. Cover and refrigerate the rice balls for another 20 minutes to firm up. Once they're firm, dip the rice balls in the beaten eggs and coat them with breadcrumbs. Fill a large pot with about 4 inches of canola oil and heat it to 350°F. Fry the arancini until they're golden and crispy, 5 to 6 minutes. Drain them on paper towels.

SHKIAFFING IT TOGETHER

In a medium-sized bowl mix the granulated sugar with 3 tablespoons of cinnamon. Toss the freshly fried arancini in the sugar-cinnamon mixture to coat.

GROCERY LIST

- 3 egg yolks
- ¼ cup raw sugar
- 1 cup heavy cream
- ½ a vanilla bean, seeds separated from pod
- 1½ cups leftover cooked white rice, cold
- ½ cup raisins, roughly chopped
- 3¼ tbsp ground cinnamon
- ¼ tsp ground nutmeg
- 3 eggs, beaten
- dry breadcrumbs
- canola oil, for deep-frying
- 1 cup granulated sugar

GEAR

- 2 medium mixing bowls
- small saucepan
- large mixing bowl
- large pot
- deep-frying thermometer

community chapter

We owe it all to our community. When we created *Bitchin' Kitchen* everyone told us we were crazy. They said that food television would never have us because there was too much edgy comedy in the show, and that comedy television would never have us because there was too much freakin' food.

Enter the *Bitchin' Kitchen* fan base. Our fans, all of you, proved them wrong. We showed the world that there were millions who weren't being served by vanilla cooking shows. Millions who were hungry for double-dark chocolate with fleur de sel. We're more than a cooking show. We're an attitude: You don't need to be plain to be palatable. You don't need to be a ditz to be hot. You don't need to be a Michelin chef to make a Bitchin' meal, and you certainly don't need to be a food snob to enjoy one. We're bringing together young and old, newbies and kitchen divas alike, and teaching a whole new generation how to grab life by the bra strap and rock their kitchens.

If it weren't for our Fierce Foodie Fans, we wouldn't have a hit TV show, two cookbooks, or a stinkin' T-shirt. *Bitchin' Kitchen is* our community. And that's why every day we entertain you online — from live chats, to supper clubs, to just having fun wasting time on your boss's dime — and we want you to know that we're forever grateful for your rockin' 'tude, your voice, and your support. (Even those who type in ALL CAPS :P.)

Because celebrity 2.0 is a two-way street, this chapter is not only dedicated to our community, but the recipes are actually written by our community! We held a nationwide recipe contest, and let me tell you, it wasn't easy picking the winners. The competition was fierce! From spicy cioppino, to bacon chocolate chip cookies, to Cajun soft-shell crabs, man, did we ever *shkoff… But there could only be five winners, and these next recipes rose to the top.

In the next coupla pages you'll also get a taste of the action that goes down in our www-world: the best comments, our community's creativity, and general kookiness. We hope that this little slice of immortality lets you know how much we really do love you. Because we do. Because you f@cking rock.

brent's twice-baked squash

Recipe by Brent Miller: "Alright. I had just got outta the Marine Corps and came to visit friends back where I was stationed. They wanted to try something new for Christmas dinner so I pulled this outta my head. It was an instant fan favorite. It even got my buddy Mikey — who hates squash — to empty his squash shell. Nothing complements a beer bird turkey as awesomely as this dish, FYI."

servings: 4 as main, 8 as a side | easy

SQUASH

Preheat the oven to 400°F. Place the whole squash on a large baking sheet and cook until the shells are slightly tender to the touch, 1 hour to 1 hour and 20 minutes. Remove the squash and turn the oven temperature down to 350°F. When the squash are cool enough to handle, cut them in half widthwise and remove the seeds. Then delicately scoop the flesh out of the squash, leaving a thin layer of flesh to help the shells stay intact. Set the flesh aside in a bowl and put the shells on a large baking sheet.

STUFFING

In a large nonstick pan melt the butter over medium-high heat and sauté the squash flesh, ham, onion, garlic, cumin, thyme, and ½ teaspoon of rosemary until the onion is translucent, about 5 minutes. Season the stuffing with the sea salt and freshly ground pepper.

SHKIAFFING IT TOGETHER

In a medium mixing bowl toss together the breadcrumbs and the two grated cheeses. Divide the sautéed mixture equally among the 4 squash shells. Lay 3 slices of pepper Jack cheese over each stuffed squash. Sprinkle the top with the breadcrumb and cheese mixture and then the remaining ½ teaspoon rosemary. Return the stuffed squash to the oven and bake until the cheeses have melted and are slightly golden, about 30 minutes. Let the stuffed squash cool for 5 minutes before serving.

GROCERY LIST

- 2 medium winter squash, such as butternut or Hubbard
- 2 tbsp unsalted butter
- 8 oz ham, cut into small dice
- 1 medium onion, cut into small dice
- 3 garlic cloves, finely chopped
- ½ tsp ground cumin
- ¼ tsp finely chopped fresh thyme
- 1 tsp finely chopped fresh rosemary
- ½ tsp sea salt
- ¼ tsp freshly ground black pepper
- 2 cups fresh breadcrumbs
- 2 cups shredded cheddar cheese
- 2 cups shredded mozzarella cheese
- 12 slices jalapeño Monterey Jack cheese

GEAR

- large baking sheet
- large nonstick pan
- medium mixing bowl

rhea's tofu piccata

Recipe by Rhea Parsons: "Who says that people with dietary limitations can't enjoy a decadent meal? To hell with them! My version of the classic Italian dish, usually made with veal or chicken, is vegan and gluten-free, but it is bursting with flavor. Cooked in a delicious sauce of vegan butter, white wine, parsley, garlic, lemons, and capers… nothing is sacrificed in this amazing dish. Panos, take the day off!"

servings: 4 | easy

TOFU

Cut the tofu block in half widthwise and then cut each half block into 4 equal slices, about ½ inch thick. In a shallow dish combine the chickpea flour, salt, and pepper. Coat both sides of the tofu slices with the seasoned flour.

Heat the oil in a large nonstick pan over medium-high heat. Sauté the tofu slices until they are browned and a bit crisp on both sides, about 4 minutes per side. Transfer the tofu to a platter and set aside.

SAUCE

Add the wine to the pan and then add the garlic. Cook until the pan is dry and the garlic is slightly golden. Quickly add the stock, lemon juice, and capers. Let the sauce cook for 1 minute, and then return the tofu slices to the pan. Cook for another minute, allowing the tofu slices to soak in the flavors of the liquid. Transfer the tofu slices back to the platter.

Add the vegan butter and 8 lemon slices to the pan. Once the butter has melted remove the pan from the heat and give the sauce a quick stir.

SHKIAFFING IT TOGETHER

Pour the sauce over the tofu slices. Garnish the platter with the parsley and the remaining fresh lemon slices.

Serve with any side dish you desire. I heated a pan with a mix of oil and vegan butter. Then I cooked some fingerling potatoes with salt, pepper, and rosemary. I let them cook until they were brown and crispy on both sides. Decadent! Tofu Piccata and fingerling potatoes are a perfect duo!

GROCERY LIST

- 1 block extra-firm tofu (approximately 18oz)
- ¼ cup chickpea flour
- ¼ tsp sea salt
- ¼ tsp freshly ground pepper
- 1 tbsp canola oil
- ¼ cup vegan white wine
- 3 garlic cloves, minced
- 1 cup low-sodium vegetable stock
- 2 tbsp fresh lemon juice
- 1 tbsp capers
- 2 tbsp vegan butter
- 12 lemon slices
- 2 tbsp finely chopped flat-leaf parsley

GEAR

- shallow dish
- large nonstick pan
- serving platter

cheri's apple cherry pork loin

Recipe by Cheri Dawn Hartman: "With our family's love of cooked pig, I have been experimenting with methods for mixing various pork products. This recipe is great smoked in an Orion Cooker with or without beer brining."

servings: 4 | intermediate

STUFFING

Preheat the oven to 400°F. Put the apple rings, dried cherries, and croutons in a food processor and pulse until crumbly with some large pieces remaining. Add the egg, salt, pepper, sage, and parsley to the food processor and pulse a few more times to blend.

ROAST

Lay the pork loin onto a large cutting board, and with a meat tenderizer pound the loin flat until approximately ½ inch thick, and enjoy this release for the day's frustrations. Spread the stuffing evenly over the loin. Roll the loin tightly along its length. Secure the loin with the bacon slices, then secure each bacon slice with a toothpick. Once done the pork loin roast will look like a spine made of pork. Place the pork loin roast on a parchment-lined baking sheet.

Cook the pork loin roast in the oven for about 50 minutes or until an instant read thermometer reads 145°F. The bacon will be slightly crispy. Let the roast rest for 5 minutes.

SAUCE

While the pork loin roast is resting, melt the butter in a small saucepan and add the jam and the vinegar. Whisk to blend. Bring the sauce to a boil and cook until it has thickened slightly, 3 to 5 minutes.

SHKIAFFING IT TOGETHER

Gently remove the toothpicks from the pork loin roast and slice the roast into 8 medallions. Place 2 on each plate and drizzle with the sauce.

GROCERY LIST
- ½ cup dried apple rings
- ½ cup dried sour cherries
- 1 cup croutons
- 1 large egg
- ¼ tsp sea salt
- ¼ tsp freshly ground black pepper
- ½ tsp roughly chopped fresh sage
- 1 tbsp roughly chopped flat-leaf parsley
- 1 boneless pork loin
- 9 thick-cut bacon slices
- 2 tbsp unsalted butter
- ¼ cup blackberry jam or jalapeño-spiked cherry jam
- ¼ cup white balsamic vinegar

GEAR
- food processor
- meat tenderizer
- 9 toothpicks
- parchment paper
- baking sheet
- instant-read thermometer
- small saucepan
- whisk

suzette's mini beef wellingtons

Recipe by Suzette Ballew: "This Bitchin' version of Beef Wellington has attitude, and will have even the most reserved Brit dancing in the streets!"

servings: 4 | intermediate

ROASTED GARLIC

Preheat the oven to 400°F. Cut ¼ inch off the top of the head of garlic, exposing the cloves. Center the garlic in aluminum foil, drizzle with 1 teaspoon of olive oil, and seal it. Bake in the center of the oven for 30 minutes. Cool, then squeeze the roasted garlic cloves out of their skins and set aside.

FILET MIGNON

Sprinkle each filet liberally with sea salt and pepper. Heat 1 teaspoon of butter and 1 teaspoon of olive oil in a large nonstick pan over medium-high heat. Sear the filets for 3 minutes on each side. Remove from the pan, cover, and chill for 20 minutes in the fridge.

SAUCE

To the large nonstick pan add 1 tablespoon of butter. Sauté the mushrooms over medium-high heat for 3 minutes, stirring frequently, until slightly browned. Remove the mushrooms, and set aside. Deglaze the pan with 1 cup of brandy. Add the roasted garlic and stir to blend, and incorporate any crispy bits. Reduce the brandy by half, about 2 to 3 minutes. Add another tablespoon of butter, the brown sugar, and whisk to dissolve. Then whisk in the cream and add the sautéed mushrooms. Reduce the heat to medium, and simmer for 5 to 7 minutes, until the sauce has thickened. Remove sauce from the heat and season with sea salt and pepper to taste. Whisk in 1 tablespoon of brandy. Strain the mushrooms from the sauce and transfer the sauce to a small saucepan. Return the mushrooms to the large pan, and sauté over medium heat until slightly caramelized, about 3 minutes. Set them aside.

SHKIAFFING IT TOGETHER

In a small bowl, beat together the egg yolk and water. Roll out the chilled puff pastry on a lightly floured surface into 14 x 14 inches. Cut four 7 x 7-inch squares. In the center of each square place 2 slices of pancetta, one fourth of the mushrooms, 1 tablespoon of Gorgonzola, and a filet. Brush the borders of each pastry square with the egg wash, then fold it over the filets as if wrapping a package. Once sealed, turn them over seam-side down on a parchment-lined baking sheet. Lightly score each Wellington, and brush with egg wash. Bake until they've reached an internal temperature of 135°F for rare, about 20 minutes. Let them rest for 5 minutes. Drizzle four plates with sauce, and then add the Wellingtons. Garnish with chives.

GROCERY LIST

- 1 head garlic
- 2 tsp olive oil
- 4 6-oz filet mignons
- sea salt & freshly ground black pepper
- 2 tbsp + 1 tsp unsalted butter
- 2 cups thinly sliced shitake mushroom caps
- 1 cup + 1 tbsp brandy
- ¾ teaspoon brown sugar
- 2 cups heavy cream
- 1 egg yolk
- 1 tbsp water
- flour, for dusting surface
- 1 lb puff pastry or 4 pre-rolled 7" x 7" sheets puff pastry, thawed if frozen, cold
- 8 slices pancetta
- ¼ cup Gorgonzola cheese, diced
- chives, finely chopped

GEAR

- foil
- large nonstick pan
- strainer
- small bowl
- basting brush
- rolling pin
- parchment paper
- instant-read thermometer

angela's chocolate almond crepes

Recipe by Angela Grujicic: "I'm always on the quest to make guilty pleasures seem healthy to me, while remaining delicious to my boyfriend — who has the palate of an 8-year-old. The whole wheat flour is healthy, flax meal provides Omega 3s, the cocoa powder has antioxidants, and the sugar is good for my sanity. But hey, if you're allergic to healthy, use regular ol' all-purpose flour, omit the flax, and enjoy your new spare tire!

servings: eight 10-inch crepes | intermediate

CREPE BATTER

Combine all the dry ingredients in a large bowl. Add the wet ingredients to the dry ingredients, and whisk until all the ingredients are moistened. Feel free to get all OCD and overmix! For hard-core OCDers who want every molecule distributed evenly, mix the wet ingredients together before you add them to the dry ingredients.

Your batter should be thin, but not runny. If it's not, add a tablespoon of water at a time until it looks right. It's not a big deal if it's too thick — just call them pancakes and get on with your life. Stick the batter in the fridge for 10 minutes until it thickens a bit. While you're waiting, stick the largest nonstick pan you have on medium heat.

Spray your pan with cooking spray, but not too much…the pan is nonstick, duh. Make sure the pan is hot enough by sprinkling a little water in the pan. It will sizzle if it's ready to go. Ladle about ¼ cup of crepe batter into your pan, and tilt and rotate the pan to spread the batter evenly across pan. Cook for 1 to 2 minutes or until the crepe is crispy around the edges, and then slide the spatula under it to free it from the pan and flip it. If you're super cool and have skills I don't have, you can flip without a spatula. Alternatively, if you're drunk and think you can pull it off, go for it. The worst that can happen is that you'll end up eating it off the floor later in the night. Don't worry, you'll likely black that part out anyways. Cook the second side for about a minute. Repeat with the remaining batter.

SHKIAFFING IT TOGETHER

Now fill your crepes with whatever you have in the pantry. Sprinkle them with mini chocolate chips when they are hot, dust them with powdered sugar, or just be creative! I like to put some almond butter and chocolate ganache on them, but that's just me.

GROCERY LIST

- 1 cup whole-wheat pastry flour
- ½ cup almond flour
- 1 tbsp flax meal
- 1 tsp unsweetened cocoa powder
- 1 tsp sugar
- 1½ cups almond milk
- ¼ cup water
- ¼ tsp vanilla extract
- cooking spray
- possible garnishes: mini chocolate chips, powdered sugar, chocolate ganache, almond butter

GEAR

- large bowl
- whisk
- large nonstick pan
- ladle
- wide pancake spatula

Bitchin' COMMUNITY COMMENTS

Mark Patterson —Nadia you are funny beyond words! LOVE your show…you made me laugh to tears last night with your "Makeup Meal" episode. If I weren't gay & already married to my guy…I'd marry you! :) Love your recipes too!

Danette L. Williams — Honey, a lot of people who watch your show are super extra comfortable. I would buy your T-shirt if I could fit it over my left tit.

Emma Borsa — Your logo does not JUST represent *Bitchin' Kitchen*, it represents all women who love to cook and be in the kitchen, but want to shatter all Stepford 1950s homemaker stereotypes. Nadia, you've put a face to a movement that has been glued to the same spot, and now it's in motion… Keep on rockin' in the free world!

Caroline Mosel — My mother and I have bonded over your show! I love the kickass morbid aspect, and my mother loves the good ol' cooking and witty comments. Cook on, sister.

Aireen Arellano — Soooo, I have always feared the kitchen. What can I say? I grew up on takeout. After watching your badass show debut on the Cooking Channel, I have this new-found spark of cooking fearlessness. So what did I do? I started cooking! I know! My mother is shocked. I am a Nadia G fan for life! THANK YOU!

Tina Rashed — My five year old son, Adam, is in love with Nadia G. He always liked helping me out in the kitchen, but after watching *Bitchin' Kitchen,* he wants to do all the cooking. You brought the chef out in both of us and we love your recipes, your style and the entire *Bitchin' Kitchen* Crew!

Audrey & Dan Grilley — Last week my daughter Audrey (age 4) showed me a drawing she made that day. I saw the logo and asked her if it was from *Pitchin' in the Kitchen* (her name for the show). So, here you go. She asks me all the time if Nadia is a rock star and I tell her yes she is. We love the show.

Food for Thought
BY EMANUEL WALL

If you've ever hung out on our fan page, you've come across Emanuel Wall's posts. He's like *Bitchin' Kitchen*'s very own Jack Handey. Here are some of his classics:

"One day the Sword fish will meet its superior the automatic semi machine gun fish. The machine gun fish will give way to the A-bomb fish, and then after that I guess we start over with regular boring lame fish. Either way fish is good."

"Socrates in his wisdom and cool looking toga once said 'Thou should eat to live, and not live to eat.' Man, when I offer quotes in a toga all I can come up with is 'Let's get this kegger party started!' "

"I am confused. If a wine-taster is a workaholic, is there a problem?"

"There is a quiet sadness when a boy realizes that he is now a man. It's nearly as sad when a Gingerbread Boy realizes that he is now a delicious Gingerbread Man."

"Deeply disturbed people are the unsung heroes of the culinary world. Honestly, it must have been a strange person that wanted to milk the first cow. Only a crazy man would want to get on raft with a pointy stick and bite into an ocean cockroach and name it lobster. To honor those crazy food visionaries the next time you happen to walk by an insane person, stop, think, raise your hand and say, 'bon appetit!'…bon appetit indeed."

"Nietzsche is known for his quote 'God is Dead.' I would like a book about his less known quotes such as 'Man am I hungry,' 'No glove no love,' and 'Come on man.' "

"I find that it helps that when you stare at the Abyss, and the Abyss stares back, to make a funny face and try and break the tension."

a word from angelique / AP

"Being *Bitchin' Kitchen's* community manager has been an epic ride. I've had the pleasure of seeing *Bitchin' Kitchen* grow from a concept to a hit show, and watched the community explode along the way. I've chatted with some of the most awesome food people around the world. I've seen fans get tattoos of our logo, create entire blogs dedicated to *Nadia G's Bitchin' Kitchen* episodes, and witnessed an impressive hunger for a new generation of lifestyle entertainment. Who knew Facebook & Twitter stalking could be so rewarding?!

"It's great getting to connect with our fans every day. We talk about everything — the show, recipes, relationships, fashion…you name it, we yap about it! I feel like I know our fans. I know who writes in ALL CAPS, I know who makes the most mouth-watering meals, and I know who posts the best comments. It's the main reason I enjoy being *Bitchin' Kitchen's* community manager so much — I know that every day there will be something fresh to chat about, and new people to virtually meet. But above all else, I love being part of a growing community that has a real passion for food, knows how to have a good time, and quite simply, RAWKS!" — *Angelique Picanco (AP)*

olive oil

We're often told to use "the best quality olive oil you can get your hands on." But what exactly is "the best quality olive oil you can get your hands on?" Virgin, extra-virgin, pretending to be a virgin…you think I'm kidding? Italian police once impounded seven olive oil production plants and arrested over forty people for shkiaffing chlorophyll into soybean and sunflower oil and trying to pass it off as extra-virgin…Sneaky.

MYTH 1 The best olive oil is cold pressed. Believe it or not, the term "cold pressed" doesn't mean anything because there's no international standard for "cold." For example, what's considered cold in Tuscany isn't what's considered cold in Alaska. And if you talk to my exes, they'll give you a whole other definition of cold.

MYTH 2 The best olive oil comes from the first pressing of the olives. With modern machinery there is no second pressing of the olives. Once the olives have been pressed, once and once alone, the goop that's left over is called "pomace," and the only way to extract oil from pomace is to add chemical solvents.

So to make a long story short: extra-virgin olive oil and virgin olive oil are the oils naturally extracted from the one and only pressing of the olives. Anything that's not labeled as extra-virgin or virgin is chemically treated, and therefore a lesser olive oil. So there you have it.

balsamic vinegar

Authentic, traditional balsamic can hail only from the provinces of Modena or Reggio Emilia in Italy. The label has to read "Aceto Balsamico Traditionale," and you'll find a big ol' Protected Designation of Origin stamp right on the bottle. ...It also costs between 100 and 400 bucks for 3 ounces. Ouch. That's because traditional balsamic isn't made from wine like most vinegars. It's made from sweet grape juice that's been reduced to a syrup called *mosto cotto,* or "grape must." This nectar of the gods is then aged anywhere from 12 to over 100 years in fancy wooden casks.

Needless to say "Aceto Balsamico Traditionale" ain't used as a salad dressing, but as a high-end condiment. Just a few drops will enhance carpaccio, aged cheeses, desserts, and your ego. The really old stuff can even be sipped after a meal like a fine scotch.

Now, the balsamic that we regularly use can be broken down into two categories: Balsamico di Modena... and rocket fuel. Balsamico di Modena is the way to go. This stuff is made in Italy from a mix of wine vinegar and *mosto cotto* — that essential grape syrup we were talking about. Then it's aged anywhere from 3 to 12 years, and at around 12 bucks a bottle this vinegar is perfect for salads, reductions, and not having to re-mortgage your house just to get a taste.

Then there's rocket fuel "balsamic." This stuff rings in at about 3 bucks a bottle, contains no *mosto cotto* whatsoever, and is loaded with artificial coloring and thickeners. Calling this stuff "balsamic" is like calling spray-can cheese "Parmigiano-Reggiano," or Nickelback a "rock band."

*italian slang dictionary

For those of you unfamiliar with Italian slang, here's a glossary of terms and Nadia-isms used in this cookbook. ⚠️ WARNING: Use with caution. This slang is extremely contagious and you may infect your friends.

All kinds: Many, a lot.
Illustrative:
Gino: "Were there lots of babes at da party?"
Tino: "Bro, all kinds."

All worried: Used sarcastically to express a lack of concern.
Illustrative:
"Me, I'm all worried about Nickelback's lawyers."

A la Prossima!: Italian for "Until next time."
Pronounciation: /ah lah pro-see-mah/
Illustrative:
"Today we cooked up 3 Bitchin' dishes that'll…

Bein Non: French-Canadian for "Of course not."
Pronunciation: /bain-no/
Illustrative:
Tina: "Bein non you can't use margarine instead of butter, bro!"

Bey yea!: An expression used to denote certainty. A substitute for "Indeed!"
Pronunciation: /bay-ya/
Illustrative:
Gino: "Did you bring da sangwiches?"
Tino: "Bey yea! My mudder made dem dis morning."

Bog: Nadsat slang for "God" in *A Clockwork Orange*, written by Anthony Burgess.
Pronunciation: /bog/
Illustrative:
Tina: "Nads, why do you say 'bog' instead of 'God'?
Nadia G: "For two reasons. 1) Sometimes I feel the need to show off a sophomoric literary intelligence. 2) I tried thanking unicorns in 2007, and people looked at me funny."

Boh: Used when one doesn't know the answer to a question, meaning "I have no idea."
Pronunciation: /bo/
Illustrative:
Frank: "Where did Mary go?"
Tony: "Boh. How should I know?"

Bourdell: Italian dialect for "bordello," meaning "chaos."
Pronunciation: /boor-dell/
Illustrative:
Mother: "Tino! Clean your room! It's a bourdell!"

Bro: Short for "brother," used to greet everyone, regardless of gender.
Illustrative:
Gino: "Bro, how's it going?"
Mary: "I'm good, bro."

Brutta figura: To make a bad impression, to disgrace. This is an Italian's greatest fear... besides removing the plastic covering from a new couch.
Pronunciation: /brute-ah fig-oo-ra/
Illustrative:
Mother: "You better hide your tattoos at the wedding or you're gonna make a brutta figura!"

Cac: Crap, low quality, not good.
Pronunciation: /cack/
Illustrative:
"Pfft! You call dat cac an espresso?!!"

Capisce: Italian for "Understand?"
Pronunciation: /ka-peesh/
Illustrative:
"I don't care about your baby pictures, capiche?"

Casalinga: Rustic, home-style Italian cooking. No fancy plating, big portions, grandma-licious.
Pronunciation: /kaza-lyn-gah/
Illustrative:
"Screw the decorative rosemary sprig! I wanna eat some old-school casalinga food!"

Che cazzo?!: WTF?!
Pronunciation: /kay cats-oh/
Illustrative:
"Che kazzo?! You're an hour late!"

Common mispronunciations:
Note that the sound for "th" does not exist in Italian slang. It is always replaced with a "d" or omitted altogether.
Illustrative:
Da: The
Dat: That
Dem: Them
Den: Then
Dey: They
Deez: These
Der/ Dair: There, They're
Dose: Those
Dis: This
Nutting: Nothing
Ting: Thing
Tink: Think
Togedder: Together
Tree: Three
Troot: Truth
Tru: Through

Dishkombomballated: Messed up, drugged, or hungover.
Pronunciation: /dish-come-bomb-ba-lated/
Illustrative:
"When I woke up after dat party, I was totally dishkombomballated."
Dizgraziate: A disgrace.
Pronunciation: /deez-grats-yea'd/
Illustrative:
"You call dat al dente?!…Dizgraziate."

Estie: French-Canadian expletive.
Pronunciation: /es-tee/
Illustrative:
"Yey! The Canadians won game 6! It's time to riot, estie."

Kerfuffled: Flustered.
Pronunciation: /ker-fuffled/
Illustrative:
"When my mom first saw Hans, she was kerfuffled."

Ma: A word of many definitions:
1. Short for "Mother."
2. Short for "mannaggia" — an Italian term meaning "Damn it."
3. The Italian equivalent of "But."
4. A great way to begin any sentence.
5. A sound that expresses annoyance when words fail.
Illustrative:
Gino: "Ma, where's da tomatoes?!" (1)
Mother: "Ma, you idiot! Der right dair in da fridge!" (2)
Gino: "Ma I looked in da fridge!" (3)
Mother: "Ma, look again!" (4)
Gino: "Maaaa." (5)

Ma please!: A sarcastic turn of phrase that expresses disbelief. The equivalent of "No way!" or "Get out of here!"
Illustrative:
Tino: "Bro, yesterday I had a threesome!"
Gino: "Ma please! Using both hands doesn't count."

Mannaggia la miseria: Italian for "damn the misery." Commonly used to express exasperation.
Pronounciation: /mah-nadge-ee-ya lah miz-air-cc-ya/
Illustrative:
"Whaddya mean Anne Burrell is coming out with a cookbook at the same time as us? Mannagia la miseria, we'll never get on the *Today Show!*"

Marone: Italian-American pronunciation of "Madonna." Used exactly like one would use the term "Jesus."
Pronounciation: /Ma-rone/
Illustrative:
"Did you see those studded heels G wore in last night's episode? Marone, I gotta get me a pair."

Me I: A self-important, redundant way to begin any sentence that would otherwise begin with "I."
Illustrative:
"Me I love The Kills!"

Mezze i piede: Infringing on your space. Literal translation: "in between my feet."
Pronunciation: /meds E pee-ate/
Illustrative:
"Get out of the kitchen when I'm cooking, you're always mezze i piede!"

Mi: Abbreviation of "minchia." To be used at the beginning of a sentence to accentuate your forthcoming statement.
Pronunciation: /me/
Illustrative:
"Mi! Me too I love cannolis!"

Minchia: A Sicilian swear word for male genitalia. Depending on your tone, it can be used as an exclamation of surprise, excitement, happiness, anger, sadness, introspection…It is as versatile as "F@ck."
Pronunciation: /meang'ya/
Illustrative:
"Minchia! I can't believe it's not butter!"

Mudder: Mother.
Illustrative:
Tino: "Bro, you're thirty-five years old and still living with your mudder!"
Gino: "So are you!"
Tino: "I know."
Gino: "So what's your point, bro?!"
Tino: "I dunno bro, I tink I was just acting tough. I'm sorry. Hold me."

Musholite: Slang for "mushy." Can be used to describe a texture or a person's character.
Pronunciation: /moosh-o-leet/
Illustrative:
Daughter: "Ma, deez beans are all musholite!"
Mother: "At least der not as musholite as your husband!"

Newrd: Nadia G's infamous pronunciation of the word "nerd." Usually used as a term of endearment, but can sometimes be used as a gentle insult due to its undeniably cute sound.
Pronunciation: /newrd/
Illustrative:
"After a quick break, we'll plate this cheesecake and talk quantum physics…Ma, whaddya think we're gonna do?! We're gonna shkoff, you newrdz!"

Nonna: Grandmother.
Pronunciation: /no-na/
Illustrative:
"Every Sunday my Nonna would give me anise candy and twenty bucks."

Nonno: Grandfather.
Pronunciation: /no-no/
Illustrative:
"Nonno would cut the cantaloupe and mumble a lot."

Pashquale: A random Italian name that can replace "Buddy."
Pronouciation: /pash-kwa-leh/
Illustrative:
"Hold it right there Pashquale… Nadia G so does not have hair extensions."

Ribambite: A derogatory term to describe someone who isn't the sharpest knife in the drawer.
Pronunciation: /ree-bam-beat/
Illustrative:
"In 2007 when I told the networks that *Bitchin' Kitchen* was both a comedy show and a cooking show, they just stared at me, all ribambite."

Salam: Slang for "salami," used to describe an actual salami sausage or an idiot.
Pronunciation: /sa-lam/
Illustrative:
"Stop hogging all da salam, you salam!"

Sciapite: Weak in flavor.
Pronunciation: /shah-peed/
Illustrative:
"You didn't use enough salt — this sauce is sciapite!"

Scraggler: An undesirable person, a hanger-on.
Illustrative:
Wife: "Why da hell is Vincenzo always at our house?! He's such a scraggler!"
Husband: "For crying out loud! He's our two-year-old son!"

Shkeefoso, Shkeef: "It sucks" or "It stinks." Can be used as a verb or an adjective.
Pronunciation: /sh-key'f/
Illustrative:
Mary: "I can't eat gizzards or tripe, it shkeefs me."
Gina: "Never mind tripe, Nickelback fa shkeef."

Shkiaff: Slang for "slap."
Pronunciation: /sh-key-ah'f/
Illustrative:
1. "If you don't stop bugging me I'm gonna give you a coupla shkiaff!"
2. "Stop fussing over presentation! Just shkiaff some pasta on the plate, I'm too hungry!"

Shkiaffing it together: Slang for "slapping it together." This is Nadia G's alternative to classic presentation and plating.
Pronunciation: /sh-key-ah'fing/
Illustrative:
"Now that the sauce is ready, we'll be straining the pasta and shkiaffing it together."

Shkiatt: Slang for "explode."
Pronunciation: /sh-key-at/
Illustrative:
Tino: "Gino, I ate tree plates of gnocchi! I felt like I was gonna shkiatt!"

Shkoff: To eat wholeheartedly; to pig out.
Pronunciation: /sh-koff/
Illustrative:
Gino: "Pfft. Bro, tree plates of gnocchi, dat's nutting! I shkoffed four plates."

Shquiblets: G-speak for anything small and cute.
Pronunciation: /Sh-quib-lets/
Illustrative:
"Although your newborn shquiblet is cute, baby poop consistency isn't riveting dinner conversation."

Stinkpod: Both an insult and a term of endearment… at the same time.
Illustrative:
"I love you, Stinkpod!"

Stu cazze: A Italian expletive used to denote sarcasm and disdain.
Pronunciation: /stew-cats/
Illustrative:
Troll: "Nads, you should really curl your fingers in when when you chop."
Nadia G: "Stu cazze curl my fingers in. I like to live on the edge."

Teet: Mispronunciation of "teeth."
Pronunciation: /teat/
Illustrative:
"I'm gonna punch you in da teet!"

Tsaketa: Nadia G's take on the obligatory TV chef tagline or catch phrase. A sound effect similar to "Bam" or "Yum-o," but more Bitchin'.
Pronunciation: /ts-sack-it-ta/
Illustrative:
"Now that we've got all our ingredients lined up, Tsaketa! Let's get cooking."

Ya okay!: Sarcastic expression that means "Yeah right!"
Illustrative:
Gino: "When Tino told me his sister was adopted, I was like: Ya okay! She has the exact same mustache."

Yammena: Italian slang for "let's go."
Pronunciation: /yeah-meh-nah/
Illustrative:
Nadia: "Crap, that is Immigration! Yammena, get the Spice Agent outta here!"

Yella: Arabic for "let's go."
Pronunciation: /yell-ah/
Illustrative:
Spice Agent: "I think that is Immigration, yella, let's get out of here."

You're gonna die: Creepy abbreviation for "You're going to die of laughter."
Illustrative:
"You've never seen *Wonder Showzen*?! Bro, you've gotta rent it, you're gonna die!"

Zia: Italian for "aunt."
Pronunciation: /zee-ya/
Illustrative:
Nadia G: "When I was a kid I used to tease my zia about her weight. With great patience she'd say: 'T'impicca come una capra.' …Direct translation: 'I'll hang you like a baby goat.' Since this would only make me laugh, she'd have to pull out the big guns and threaten to never feed me one of her famous sausages again. Now that had me backpeddling, fast. What can I say? It's an Italian thing."

index

Notes

Credits

NADIA G'S BITCHIN' KITCHEN
Created by NADIA GIOSIA and JOSHUA DORSEY

Nadia G — NADIA GIOSIA
Panos the Fishguy — PETER KOUSSIOULAS
Spice Agent — BEN SHAOULI
Hans — BART ROCHON

COOKIN' FOR TROUBLE
Written by NADIA GIOSIA
Spice Agent segments written with BEN SHAOULI
Book Design, Style, and Concept by NADIA GIOSIA
Assistant Graphic Designer SHIREL REVAH jackalopedesigns.com
Recipe Creation Assistance by GIOSIA FAMILY, DORSEY FAMILY, TIFFANY RIEDER stylisteculinaire.ca
Produced and Directed by JOSHUA DORSEY
Production Coordinator MELISSA MALKIN
Web Team and Community Chapter Coordinators ANGELIQUE PICANCO, NICOLA HYDE,
ELA MISZKURKA, ISABEL CAFARO

THEMATIC PHOTOGRAPHY
Chapters 3-8 & 10-16 + Hans, Panos, Spice Agent:
MARIANNE LAROCHELLE
mariannelarochelle.com

Cover + chapters 1, 2 & 9:
MARTIN TREMBLAY lepinch.com

Hair & Makeup: SANDRA TRIMARCO

Art Direction: PAOLA RIDOLFI

Head Stylists for cover + chapters 1, 2 & 9:
PASCAL & JEREMIE pjconcept.com
Onset stylist: CHRISTINE LAGANIERE
Additional Styling: SANDRA TRIMARCO

Graphic FX for cover, chapters 1 & 9 + Hans, Panos,
Spice Agent: VISUAL BOX levisualbox.com
Graphic FX for chapters 2 & 9:
MATHIEU LEVESQUE mathieulevesque.com

Asst to M.Larochelle: GILGAMESH POLUX FUICA
Asst to Martin Tremblay: YANNIK FOURNIER
Asst to Sandra Trimarco: CHANTAL ST. ARNAUD
CHIZU ISHIZUKA
Asst to Paola Ridolfi: ADAM FRAPPIER,
BRIGITTE TURBIDE, MARIE-CLAUDE GUAY
PAs: ISABEL CAFARO, AMANDA GARQUE

FOOD PHOTOGRAPHY
Food Photographer:
RYAN SZULC ryanszulc.com

Food Stylist:
NOAH WITENOFF nustyling.com

Prop Stylist:
MADELEINE JOHARI
PAOLA RIDOLFI

Coordinator:
CINZIA RUFFOLO

Recipe Testing:
TIFFANY RIEDER
NOAH WITENOFF

Assistant Food Stylist:
CHRISTELLE DUTREMBLE

Assistant to Ryan Szulc:
MATT GIBSON

FONTS

Vinegar ©2008 by TJARDA KOSTER/
JELLOWEEN FONT FOUNDRY

Artistamp Medium ©FONT BROTHERS
fontbros.com

Gf Ordner Normal ©1998 LORENZ
GOLDNAGL of Gfonts

Indoctrine ©JORDAN LLOYD

Bambi ©GERARD E. BERNOR.

Reservoir Grunge © ZETAFONTS a franke
foundry.

Loki Cola ©1999 DALE THORPE
utopiafonts

Porcelain ©MISPRINTED TYPE
misprintedtype.com

Neon Lights ©ALLEN R. WALDEN

ARTWORK

Digital Painting on p. 188 JODEE ROSE

Grunge Texture Brushes on p. 132/3
©JASON GAYLOR

Smoke Brushes on p. 130 ©FALLN-
BRUSHES

Cookware Collage Background on p. 38
MARC GAGNON

Pasta Bustier on Cover: Concept: NADIA G
Execution: PASCAL & JÉRÉMIE

Leather Harness on Pigs: PRIAPE in collaboration with PASCAL &
JÉRÉMIE

SPONSORS

ELMIRA STOVEWORKS elmirastoveworks.com
BETSEY JOHNSON
D&G
MAISON LA CORNUE maisonlacornue.ca
ARES KITCHEN AND BAKING SUPPLIES arescuisine.com
BOUTIQUE EVA B eva-b.ca
Latex Jumpsuit by POLYMORPHE polymorphe.com
Bacon Apron by DOTS DINERS etsy.com/shop/dotsdiner
Bacon fabric by VO spoonflower.com/fabric/361183
Angel fabric by NALO HOPKINSON spoonflower.com/profiles/nalo_
hopkinson.
Mexican Oil Cloths by DENVER FABRICS denverfabrics.com

Thanks

It takes a community to raise a cookbook: from the famiglia's recipes, to the dedicated team of artists and producers that come together to turn pixel dust to paper, to the rock-solid Bitchin' Crew, and for the first time, our Bitchin' web community at large that inspired and contributed!

Let's start with the family because this book features so many of their delectable recipes inspired by garlic and love. Thanks to mamma LUISA GIOSIA, mamma TANJA DORSEY, grandma DOROTHY DORSEY, ZIA MIMI & ZIO PIERRE BOIVIN, ZIA MARIANNA & ZIO PIETRO, TERRI GIOSIA, and ROSEANNA & FRANK MIGNIACCA. A very special thanks to STEPHEN DORSEY for being the ultimate consiglieri year-round, and a special shout-out to our youngest photography critics: JILLIAN & LAUREN, VALERIE & VICTORIA. Big thanks to TIFFANY RIEDER for all her contributions, and to INGRID and MERCY for knowing how things go down in the kitchen.

Big props to all the brilliant artists that worked with us: MARIANNE LAROCHELLE for her stunning thematic photography of Nadia G and Crew, RYAN SZULC and his team for the next-level food photography, NOAH WITENOFF for styling that food so deliciously fine, MARTIN TREMBLAY for raising the bar with pigs & parquet, PASCAL & JÉRÉMIE for helping us reach that bar with gusto 'en masse', SHIREL REVAH for helping make the design of this book a reality, and finally to my oldest collaborator, SANDRA TRIMARCO, for her endless inspiration with hair and makeup that keeps us both from a life of crime, bro.

I'd like to thank GUY FIERI for believing in us, and taking us under his firecracker wings. Big ups to REID STRATHEARN & THE GRAND KREW for supporting Bitchin' Kitchen through thick and thin. And a humble thank you to MICHAEL PSALTIS – the P SALT of the earth – for all the excitement of the deal, his commitment, tireless hard work, and patience during this project.

Huge thanks to rockstar editor-at-large PAMELA CANNON and everyone at BALLANTINE & RANDOM HOUSE for making this book happen: MELISSA POSSICK, JANE VON MEHREN, GREG MORTIMER, MARK MAGUIRE, SUSAN CORCORAN and ASHLEY GRATZ-COLLIER. (I still can't believe we have a book published by freakin' Random House!!! *Miiiiii.)

Epic thanks to COOKING CHANNEL for dishing out the next generation of lifestyle entertainment, and giving us a home in the US of A. You rock BROOKE JOHNSON, BRUCE SEIDEL, MICHAEL SMITH, SUSIE FOGELSON, and the whole SCRIPPS family!

Mille Grazie to LESLIE MERKLINGER at FOOD NETWORK CANADA for being our fairy godmother. Big thanks to TRICON FILMS for helping make our dreams of going from net to network a reality: SHAAM MAKAN, ANDREA GORFOLOVA, JAMEEL BHARMAL and CARRIE MUDD.

Massive thanks to the BROOKS GROUP for putting us on the map. Big love to: REBECCA BROOKS, NIKI TURKINGTON, ERIKA MARTINEAU, AMANDA SANTORO, KERI LARSON, MARISSA FLORINDI, and all the BROOKETTES past and present.

Thanks TOM SARIG for seeing the rock star in us, for all the dedication and support, and for introducing us to LOU REED. (I grew up listening to the Velvet Underground, to get a quote from an idol is unbelievable.) Huge thanks to LOU REED for forever inspiring generations to take a walk on the wild side.

Thanks ADAM NETTLER at CAA for the sound counsel, and excitement for all things Bitchin'.

High-five to da Bitchin' Boyz: the hilarious BEN SHAOULI, the larger-than-life PETER KOUSSIOULAS, and the ripped BART ROCHON (who's hotter than scotch bon-ettes.)

*Tsaketa to my passionate web crew: my main girl and community manager ANGELIQUE PICANCO – who's been there from the beginning and rocks the interwebs like no other, along with ISABEL CAFARO, ELA MISZKURKA, and NIKI HYDE.

Thanks to BRIAN HENDRICKS at ELMIRA STOVEWORKS for rockin' our kitchen since day one. Thanks to MELISSA MALKIN for supporting all the way through, for realz. Thanks to MICHAEL SYMON and DEBI MAZAR for being kindred spirits.

Massive W00T, W00T to our WEB COMMUNITY for making it all worthwhile, for the overwhelming number of awesome submissions for our community chapter, and for being there every day to entertain us as much as we entertain you.

I'd like to thank my superman and partner in crime JOSHUA DORSEY, without whom none of this would have been possible. We survived the BNG era, me and you baby, FTW.

And again, thanks from the bottom of our hearts to the whole family for all your unwavering support throughout the years, and my late Dad for naming me Sue.

COOKIN
F
TRO

About
THE AUTHOR

Nadia Giosia is the creater, writer, and host of *Nadia G's Bitchin' Kitchen*, a hit comedy-cooking show on the Cooking Channel and Food Network Canada. A pioneer of digital entertainment, she is the first woman to go from net to network in the lifestyle space. She lives in Montreal, and between you and me, can become a bit aggressive when she drinks.

BITCHINLIFESTYLE.TV
FACEBOOK.COM/BITCHINKITCHEN
TWITTER.COM/BITCHINKITCHEN
NADIAG.COM